# THE ONLY DOG TRICKS BOOK YOU'LL EVER NEED

Impress Friends, Family—
and Other Dogs!

Gerilyn J. Bielakiewicz
cofounder of Canine University®

*With contributions from*
Paul S. Bielakiewicz, Carlo DeVito, Amy Ammen,
and Kim Campbell Thornton

Adams Media
Avon, Massachusetts

Published by
Adams Media, a division of F+W Media, Inc.
57 Littlefield Street, Avon, MA 02322. U.S.A.
*www.adamsmedia.com*

ISBN 10: 1-59337-256-6
ISBN 13: 978-1-59337-256-9
Printed in the United States of America.

J   I   H   G

**Library of Congress Cataloging-in-Publication Data**
Bielakiewicz, Gerilyn J.
The only dog tricks book you'll ever need / by Gerilyn J. Bielakiewicz.
        p.        cm.
ISBN 1-59337-256-6
1. Dogs--Training. I. Title.
SF431.B4432 2005
636.7'0887—dc22
2004019232

Contains material adapted and abridged from *The Everything® Dog Training and Tricks Book*, by Gerilyn J. Bielakiewicz, ©2003, Adams Media. Some additional material also excerpted and abridged from *The Everything® Golden Retriever Book* by Gerilyn J. Bielakiewicz and Paul S. Bielakiewicz, ©2004, F+W Publications, Inc.; *The Everything® Dog Book* and *The Everything® Puppy Book*, by Carlo DeVito and Amy Ammen, ©1999 and ©2003, Adams Media; and *The Everything® Labrador Retriever Book* by Kim Campbell Thornton, ©2004, F+W Publications, Inc.

This publication is designed to provide accurate and authoritative information with regard to the subject matter covered. It is sold with the understanding that the publisher is not engaged in rendering legal, accounting, or other professional advice. If legal advice or other expert assistance is required, the services of a competent professional person should be sought.
        —From a *Declaration of Principles* jointly adopted by a Committee of the American Bar Association and a Committee of Publishers and Associations

Many of the designations used by manufacturers and sellers to distinguish their products are claimed as trademarks. Where those designations appear in this book and Adams Media was aware of a trademark claim, the designations have been printed with initial capital letters.

Interior photographs by Karen Hocker Photography.

*This book is available at quantity discounts for bulk purchases.*
*For information, please call 1-800-289-0963.*

# Contents

# Introduction

Usually, when we think of dog training, we think of teaching our dogs to respond to necessary commands and developing basic obedience. Without a doubt, these sorts of things are the essential building blocks for a well-trained dog. But training doesn't stop once a dog has mastered Sit, Stay, Come, and Heel. Beyond these familiarities, there are a wide variety of tricks we can help our dogs to learn, not because we *have to*, but because we *want to*.

Most dog-lovers recognize the innate intelligence of their canine pals. The more time you put into trick training, however, the more amazing this reality becomes. With time and consistent practice, you'll be astounded as you see the complex tasks your dog can handle, as her facility for understanding your verbal cues and body language grows.

People often joke about how they wish their pets would earn their keep around the house by doing something productive. Well, through trick training, you really can teach your dog to retrieve her own dinner dish, pick up after herself, and even fetch and find things for you.

But let's not forget the fun in all this. After all, fun is ultimately the reason why we teach our dogs tricks. Dogs are active, fun-loving creatures who need lots of mental stimulation as well as physical exercise. When dogs don't have enough to do or think about, they get bored, they get frustrated, they get into mischief, or—worse yet—

they become listless, depressed, sedentary, or even aggressive. Trick training is the perfect way to spice up your dog's daily routine by giving her exciting and challenging new things to learn. Dogs crave our praise and approval, and as her ability to perform tricks increases, she'll thrive.

Don't forget, this tremendous enjoyment is a two-way street— you'll be delighted, amused, excited, and proud as your pooch succeeds at mastering new tricks over time. And, although you might not realize it at first, when you're merely setting out to have some fun by teaching tricks, your best friend is becoming a smarter, more attentive, and well-behaved dog in the process.

Best of all, trick training gives your dog exactly what she craves most: quality time with you! Teaching tricks builds trust and communication, and it strengthens your relationship with each other. By learning to work together and rely on each other as a team, you'll forge a deeper, closer connection that will make a tremendous difference in both of your lives. Nothing beats the loyalty and love of a faithful canine companion, and trick training will continually enhance that bond.

So brush up on your basic training, then get ready to start training tricks. Once you get going with basic tricks, you and your dog will have such a good time you'll get hooked, and before you know it, you'll be wowing everyone you know with your performances.

If you and your pooch are in a recreational rut at home, or you've been lacking in the activity department lately, it's time to stop lounging around. You and your dog's couch-potato days are numbered.

## Chapter 1

# The Benefits of Teaching Tricks

Trick training is a must for all dog owners who think of their pets as part of the family. Performing tricks keeps old dogs young, agile, and flexible and gives young, energetic dogs an outlet for their energy. Teaching tricks is about having fun and being a little silly, but it can also greatly benefit a frustrated owner and an overactive dog. At first thought, teaching your dog to roll over, play dead, or sit up may seem somewhat frivolous—until you realize that in order to do those tricks your dog must have some basic understanding of the Sit or Lie Down command. A dog who learns to perform tricks is a more well-trained and well-behaved dog overall.

Teaching tricks capitalizes and improves upon what your dog already knows and makes it better. Tricks can help you to control a dog who barks too much or shakes and shivers when she meets new people, simply by giving her a more acceptable alternative.

Likewise, a goofy energetic dog will keep his paws off your company if he has a show-stopping Play Dead command in his repertoire. Not to mention that trick training greatly improves doggie public relations—it's a particularly effective way to win over non-dog-lovers.

In this sense, trick training is especially beneficial for larger dogs or those whose breed alone makes people nervous. A person who is afraid of dogs is likely to react much differently to a big, silly German shepherd balancing a cookie on his nose than they would to one who is just sitting politely. The more relaxed visitors are when they're around your dog, the more your dog will like having them around.

### Quick Fix: Tricks for Breaking the Ice

Large dogs can sometimes be scary to non-dog people or children. Having your dog perform a fun trick is a smart way to get people who might be feeling nervous to smile and relax instead. Play Dead and Roll Over are great for helping guests who aren't used to being around dogs to feel more comfortable.

## The Trick Is in Good Training

The beauty of teaching tricks is that you can teach them to any dog of any size, breed, or temperament. You are limited only by your dog's physical ability to perform a particular task. Before you can teach your dog any tricks, however, you must establish a strong foundation of basic training. After all, you can't expect your dog to perform a complicated trick if she can't even sit on command.

It's important to establish a good relationship with your dog from the start. Training a dog is like any other relationship; you must provide your dog with a strong leadership structure. Being your dog's leader is partly about providing your dog with rules and boundaries for what is and isn't acceptable, partly about teaching your dog what is expected of her, and partly about spending time together and learning to enjoy each other's company.

From the moment you bring your new puppy home, she is learning how to get along with your family—a species entirely different from her own. Remember, an untrained dog still learns things, just not necessarily the things you want her to know. As I often tell my students, you get what you reinforce. If you don't give her any instruction, or you're vague and inconsistent when you do instruct her, she's sure to get confused, and this confusion will result in undesirable behavior and mischief. But if you pay attention to what your dog is doing right and spend time teaching her what is expected of her, you will be rewarded with a well-mannered pet who becomes a beloved member of your family.

### Quick Fix: Keep Your Dog out of Trouble

Teaching your dog simple tricks in one- to three-minute sessions several times a day can help to alleviate boredom and create a more content dog. Giving your dog something to think about is a definite furniture saver, but it doesn't replace common sense. Be sure to use gates, crates, and pens to keep your dog from getting into trouble in your absence.

Much of your dog's training has to do with the structure you provide for her regarding what is and is not allowed. Teaching your dog the basics in the midst of various distractions and in new environments is part of being a good dog parent and will help you avoid future behavior problems. The better trained your dog is, the better relationship the two of you will share.

## Trick Training Strengthens Communication

Good training strengthens your bond with your dog, because when you are training him, you are teaching him to share a common language of words and signals. Teaching your dog the meaning of the basic obedience commands gives you a vocabulary for communicating effectively with your dog in day-to-day interactions.

As with any communication, you and your dog need to understand each other, and when you do, you'll be amazed at just how intelligent dogs are and what can be accomplished through training. Dogs who are trained to respond to basic commands are fun to own because you can direct their behavior in appropriate ways so that you will have a more enjoyable life together. Most people who train their dogs past the basics really begin to appreciate communicating with another species. Specialized training expands your bond with your dog and allows you to communicate on a higher level.

The strong bonds developed through training will carry over into tricks, play, and all other things you do with your dog. If your dog likes to swim and you like to walk on the beach, for instance, think of how much more you'll enjoy your time together if, when the walk is over, you can simply call your dog and he comes to you right away so you can leave.

## Trick Tips: Trick Training Improves Skill

Trick training will make you a better dog trainer in general, because you'll know how to motivate your dog and how to break things down into small parts. Since training your dog is a lifelong process, the more you practice the skills of a good dog trainer the better you will get at it and the more quickly your dog will learn.

Since training your dog is a lifelong process, the more you regularly practice the skills of a good dog trainer, the better you'll be, and the more quickly your dog will learn. A good dog trainer is always searching for new ways to motivate her dogs and welcomes the input of all different methods of dog training. There is no one way to train a dog. Modern dog training methods have become kinder and gentler on the dog and the human, helping you to form a stronger bond while being gentle on the dog in the process. If someone suggests a method you have strong objection to keep searching and find a better way. There are many roads that lead to a trained dog.

## Behavior Fixes

Teaching tricks can help you to be more creative about fixing behavior problems with your dog. If you take the time to evaluate why your dog is doing what she is doing, you will figure out a solution that works for you. For example, some dogs who bark when visitors come are much quieter if they are allowed to carry a toy to the visitor. Dogs who jump can learn to do a Bow or Sit and Wave in exchange for petting from guests, or do their best version of Roll Over or Play Dead if you need to relax a non-dog-person who is afraid of your large dog.

Whatever the problem, you can use tricks in place of the inappropriate behavior to redirect your dog's energy and enthusiasm. The key here is making sure that you practice the trick in all different kinds of environments with all different kinds of distractions until your dog's

Golden Retriever Waving

response to the cue is immediate and perfect. The more distraction-proof your tricks are, the more useful they will be to you when you ask the dog to do them.

## Tricks Teach Self-Control

Most people who own energetic dogs complain at some point about the dog's lack of self-control. Dogs don't just grow out of this; without training they will not one day wake up and act better behaved. If you don't put the time into training your dog to have better overall manners, you will live with a whirling dervish who never learns just to hang out with people.

Energetic dogs do have their benefits, however. Training an energetic dog is fun because they don't tire as easily as other dogs, and they are always willing to try new things. An energetic dog will go along with just about any crazy trick you can dream up—they live for attention any way they can get it. Combining a romp in the park with tricks can give your dog an awesome workout and at the same time teach him manners and self-control.

### Quick Fix: Tricks for Energetic Dogs

Dogs with lots of energy are really good at learning tricks because you can capitalize on many of the natural behaviors they offer. Little dogs love to stand on their hind legs or jump in place to see what's on the table, for instance, while big dogs like to spin in circles and stand on their hind legs to take a look out the window or to get your attention.

Performing tricks requires some measure of control on the dog's part because she has to pay attention to your cues and get feedback on what's going right. Dogs who are constantly on the move need skilled trainers who can give them lots of feedback and break the tricks down into tiny steps. Trying to push such dogs too far too fast will result in frustration for both of you. Keep in mind that teaching your dog tricks should be fun regardless of what you train him to do.

## Good Therapy

If you're still looking for more good reasons to teach your dog tricks, think about the benefits of visiting nursing homes and hospitals. Share your dog's talents with patients who may have had a dog as part of their lives at some point, but can no longer do so because of their health circumstances. These folks might really appreciate the warm, loving companionship of a well-behaved dog.

If you and your dog are visiting with patients one on one or in a group, you can use tricks to break the ice and to get people to warm up to your dog, just as you would in other circumstances. Tricks are also a great opening for conversations with patients. Dogs don't have to do much to make people happy—you'll often see everyone visibly relax and smile when they see your dog do anything remotely silly.

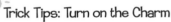

Trick Tips: Turn on the Charm
Performing tricks can improve timid people's idea of your dog, because many non-dog people perceive dogs who can perform tricks as friendlier. After all, what scaredy cat can resist a dog who says his prayers, rolls over, and plays dead?

## Tips for Improving the Trick-Training Process

The most difficult part of being a beginner is that you are also learning while you are trying to teach your dog. Be patient with yourself—dog training is a physical skill that requires lots of practice and repetition. You will reap the rewards a hundredfold the first time it all comes together and your dog performs a trick perfectly.

**Trick Tips: Never Use Force**
As you search for the right dog-training school, remember that dog training doesn't require the use of force. If you are having problems with your dog's behavior, she needs more training, not heavy-handed corrections and reprimands.

To teach tricks, you need to be able to break things down into component steps that are easily achieved in a training session. Eventually, you'll become adept at knowing how much information your dog will need in order to succeed at a given trick, and exactly when to fade out the extra help so that your dog can perform on his own. These skills come with time and practice, but there are several things you can do to help speed up the process.

**1.** Keep a notebook to record your training sessions.
**2.** Before you begin, map out the steps involved in teaching a particular trick.
**3.** Make sure your plan is flexible, and be ready to add in more detailed steps if your dog has trouble understanding what you want.
**4.** Arm yourself with the best treats and rewards to keep your dog motivated.
**5.** Time your sessions so they don't run longer than five minutes.
**6.** Use clicker training consistently to mark and reinforce good behavior: Read the details in Chapter 3 and familiarize yourself with how it works; it will save you tons of time in the long run.
**7.** Try to stick to the plan you've mapped out; don't click the dog for lots of different behaviors in one session.
**8.** If you get stuck on one particular trick, brainstorm with a friend about how to help your dog through it.
**9.** Add in distractions as soon as the dog starts to get the hang of what you're trying to teach.
**10.** Don't be afraid to backtrack and review previous steps if your dog's behavior falls apart in a new place.

In general, your dog's attitude is the best measure of your success as a trainer. If you keep sessions upbeat and fun, make it easy for your dog to succeed, and remember to end on a positive note, it won't be long before your dog thinks that working with you is better than anything else in the world.

## Consistency Is Key

Practicing on a regular basis is important if you want to become a good trainer and accomplish the goals you've established for your dog. Success will come more easily if you designate several times a week to practice tricks with your dog. This will ensure that you will have lots of opportunities to experiment with techniques, and your dog will have lots of time to get the hang of working with you. Once you consistently include training in your weekly routine (or daily routine, if your dog is young and learning the basics of living politely with humans), you will realize how easy the whole process is. You'll also appreciate how much fun it is to have a dog that works with you because she enjoys it.

### Trick Tips: Take a Trick or Agility Class

Many training schools offer more than obedience classes; some offer agility classes, tricks classes, flyball, tracking, hunting, herding, or other types of dog sports. Learning something new is more fun when you have the right tools and support—so be sure that the training school's philosophy matches your own and that you feel comfortable there.

## The Benefits of Strong Leadership

Up to this point, you've learned about the benefits of trick training, and now you've even got some trick-training tips under your belt. Before you move forward with your trick training, however, you need to understand the importance of being a strong leader to your dog. Dogs are pack animals who thrive on rules, consistency, and expectations.

Setting limits about what is allowed and how you expect them to act is not only fair, it's essential to having a healthy, well-adjusted dog. Don't worry! Being a strong, fair leader is not about being physical with your dog. A true leader would never need to pin a dog down or give a harsh correction.

Leadership isn't about forcing dogs to obey. It requires you to provide structure and establish boundaries by controlling resources. The more time you spend establishing yourself as the greatest person in your dog's life—the one who has the ability to give your dog access to everything that is important to him—the more control you will have over your dog's behavior, and the better behaved he will be. Being a strong leader is the first step toward ridding your dog of behavior problems. Following are some guidelines on how to be a strong, fair leader. (The specifics of training these basic commands will be discussed in Chapter 5.)

1. Nothing in life is free. Make sure you give your dog a job. Teach her to Sit for dinner, Lie Down before doors are opened for her, etc.

2. Humans go first through doorways and up and down stairs. This prevents your dog from escaping out the front door or knocking you down the stairs. Teach your dog to Sit and Stay until he is released through the door.

3. Down/Stay sessions for five to twenty minutes at a time help teach your dog self-control and give her a constructive job to perform around distractions and company.

4. No dogs on the beds or furniture. Young dogs should sleep in a crate or in their own bed, not in bed with you. Your bed is the highest, most special place in the house and should be reserved for you only.

5. Don't repeat a command more than once. If your dog doesn't respond on the first try, he does not get what you were offering.

6. Ignore your dog if she nudges you for attention. Leaders give attention on their own terms, not when their dogs demand it.

**7.** Ignore your dog if he is constantly pushing toys at you. Leaders initiate play and decide when the game starts and ends. This keeps a dog on his toes because he never knows when the fun begins.

**8.** Follow through. If you've asked your dog to do something but she does not respond, make sure you help her to get into the right position rather than repeating the command.

**9.** Provide consequences. Ignore what you don't like; avoid yelling at your dog for barking or jumping, for instance. From your dog's perspective, any attention is better than none, and speaking to the dog can often be mistaken for reinforcement.

Because you control the things your dog wants access to, your leadership will help you build a strong bond with your dog, convincing him that you are the key to everything he desires. Strong leadership will give you the foundation you need to teach your dog how to behave appropriately and become a welcomed member of the family. Once your dog knows how to behave, you can successfully teach him all sorts of fun tricks.

## Ten Keys to Training Success

Throughout this book, you will learn effective techniques to ensure your success as a trainer, and your dog as a student. Most "keys to success" are universal, but it will be helpful for you to think of them in terms of your pet's distinct personality.

**1.** *Be patient.* All dogs learn at different speeds and often don't grasp concepts as quickly as we think they should. Having patience with your dog will help him to be successful.

**2.** *Plan ahead.* Set your dog up to succeed. If your dog isn't "getting it," the behavior probably needs to be broken down into smaller steps.

3. *Be realistic.* Don't expect your dog to perform a behavior in an environment you haven't taught him in.

4. *Be kind.* Use positive methods to teach your dog what's expected of him.

5. *Avoid punishment.* Harsh corrections have no place in the learning phase of a dog's development. Instead, teach your dog what you want him to do.

6. *Reward effectively.* Reinforce proper behavior with what motivates your dog. A pat on the head is nice but not necessarily what he wants. Remember that this is his paycheck: Pay up!

7. *Be generous.* All new trainers tend to be cheap with rewards. Reward correct responses often and don't be afraid to reward exceptionally good responses with extra treats, praise, toys, and love.

8. *Set goals.* If you don't know where you are going and have not planned out the session, how will you know when your dog's got it?

9. *Practice often.* Teach your dog in short, frequent sessions.

10. *Stay positive.* Quit with your dog wanting more. An enthusiastic student is always an eager learner.

If you know your dog well, you will be able to choose training methods that work for both of you. You might be surprised to learn that he doesn't necessarily like or respond to all the things you assumed he would. Adjusting your teaching style can have a big impact on the success of your training program.

The simple truth of training dogs is that you get what you pay attention to. Set your dog up to succeed, limit his options, and reinforce what's going right. Soon you'll not only have a well-behaved dog, you'll have a dog who has lots of fun—and entertains everyone else—by performing all sorts of tricks.

## Trick Training Is Fun and Exciting

Trick training is something anyone can do. Getting out there and showing people how much fun it is can be a great way to educate the public about the importance of establishing a positive relationship with their dogs. Whatever your reasons for teaching tricks, the bottom line is to have fun with your dog. The tricks that follow in the successive chapters of this book are meant to get you excited about—and hooked on—training your dog. Get going now, and you'll soon see how much fun you can have teaching your pooch some new tricks.

## Chapter 2

# Know Your Dog's Personality and Needs

Before any trick training can occur, it's a good idea to get in touch with what type of personality your dog has. For instance, is she highly active, or more of a slowpoke? What kinds of rewards does she respond well to, and which sorts of activities motivate her? Finding out how your dog responds to distractions and whether she's motivated by toys or games, for example, might be helpful in putting together a training program that is easy to implement. If you take the time to evaluate why your dog does what she does, you'll find unique solutions that work for you.

Don't forget that your dog's personality is just one part of the equation. You need to address her specific needs as well. All animals have a need for food, water, and shelter, and we provide these things for our dogs with barely a second thought. However, exercise and mental stimulation are the often-overlooked needs that can mean the difference between a problem dog and a really great dog who is cooperative and well-trained. Providing adequate activity and the right foundation for learning is essential before tackling tricks. If a dog's needs for exercise, training, and attention are met and she is carefully managed according to her age and training level, you will have fewer behavioral problems to correct and, therefore, a better chance at teaching tricks successfully.

## How Well Do You Know Your Dog?

Breaking your training sessions down into small steps, learning what motivates your dog, and finding out where your dog is most distracted will help you know where to start. Below are some questions you might want to ask yourself before you begin your training program.

- Is the dog energetic or laid back? A maniac retriever or a couch potato?
- Does he do something that you've always meant to put on cue but didn't know how to?
- Is his attention span short or long? How does he respond amid distractions?
- What is his favorite treat or toy?
- Does he give up or does he persist until he gets the job done?

Understanding your dog's personality and learning style is essential to enjoyable and successful training, whether you're teaching him tricks, or anything else. Teaching an energetic dog a fast-moving, flashy trick is exciting and invigorating not only for the dog, but also for your audience. Recognizing your dog's individual tendencies and finding just the right treats, toys, and games to grab his attention will help your dog to associate training with fun and help you to achieve your training goals.

## Energy Highs and Lows

Some dogs are couch potatoes; others run circles around us all day. Differences in breed, temperament, and personality all come into play when designing a successful training program. Living with your dog makes you the expert when it comes to knowing the ins and outs of her personality and just what will work for her. Paying attention to how active your dog is can help you learn about her personality and help you to choose tricks that will be easy and fun to teach.

## Bundles of Energy

Active dogs love active tricks because they make the most of natural behaviors, such as spinning, jumping, barking, and pawing. When dogs have this much energy, take advantage of their abilities and teach appropriate tricks.

However, high-energy dogs do get overstimulated easily, and do best in short, concise training sessions with clear goals in mind. If you don't push a high-energy dog to work for long periods, they will fall in love with learning tricks.

## Pups Who Don't Have as Much Pep

Lower-energy dogs may be harder to get moving until they figure out what you want them to do. These dogs are thinkers, and they like to know where you're going with all of your instruction. Go slowly if you have a less-active dog. Also try to keep your sessions short, because these sorts of dogs often bore easily and hate repeating things too many times. Training before a meal (using unique treats as rewards) often perks them up and sparks a good session.

### Trick Tips: Working around Distractions

If you can't get your dog's attention in ten to fifteen seconds, start putting some distance between your dog and the distraction. Increasing the distance will make it easier for your dog to focus and perform an exercise. As he gains confidence and learns to pay attention, you can gradually decrease the distance without losing the behavior.

Medium-energy dogs are the easiest to work with because they are cooperative even if you make a lot of mistakes and are less organized. They don't mind repeating things over and over, and they are patient with you when you slip up or haven't planned out what you are trying to teach. Dogs with moderate energy levels are laid back and fun, turning their energy on like a rocket booster when they need to, but generally going along with whatever you're doing.

## Personality and Social Temperament

Before you begin your training program, you should also ask yourself some questions about your dog's personality traits. It can save a lot of time if you start training your dog in an environment that isn't so distracting that he can't pay attention. Teaching your dog where he is most relaxed and least distracted, or worried, will help him to be successful.

Dogs who are easily distracted because of their friendliness around people benefit from training sessions that start somewhere quiet, then quickly move on to involve the distractions they find hard to resist. Training your dog to be obedient even in the midst of distractions is one way to ensure that she will listen to your instruction when other people are around.

### Trick Tips: Making Progress

If you are willing to devote five to ten minutes of daily practice on a regular basis, both you and your dog are likely to achieve excellent results. Training a dog is a lifelong affair; it's not a means to an end, but the development of a relationship. In this regard there is never really an end to training.

Shy dogs, on the other hand, are sometimes hard to train in public until they are more confident. With this type of dog, practice in a comfortable environment first, and then gradually integrate distractions with familiar people. The ultimate goal is to incorporate strangers and new places so that your dog will be obedient anywhere.

## What Motivates Your Pooch?

Learning what rewards your dog likes is crucial to being a successful dog trainer. The reward is your dog's paycheck for playing this training game with you. It has to be something he's willing to work for, not simply something you want him to have. Some people have hangups about using food to train dogs because they think it cheapens their bond with the dog. They believe the dog should perform out of respect or love for them. Nonsense. Using food to train your dog is a way to get where you want to go. Training a dog with what he wants as a reward is both respectful to his doggy-ness and effective in the interest of time and resources.

### Trick Tips: Every Dog Is Different

If you've trained other dogs, keep in mind that dogs, like people, have different aptitudes. Just as some people have a facility for language, while others have an inclination for science, some dogs might be better at stays, while others catch on quickly to recalls.

Dogs don't perform out of love; their behavior or misbehavior has nothing to do with their love for us. Even dogs who chew the couch and bite the postman love their human families. But if you want that postman-biter to like your mail carrier, it'll probably take more than just a pat on the head as a reward to get him to cooperate.

Dogs are motivated by and will work for food, just like people work for money. We all need money to pay our bills and live our lives; dogs need food to live and enjoy theirs. Many dogs eat out of a bowl once or twice a day for free. Why not take that food and use it as a tool to train them to behave in a way that is acceptable to you? Once a dog is hooked on training and you have a good bond with her, you can use other rewards to reinforce positive, appropriate behavior. Here are some yummy ideas for treats:

- Boiled chicken
- Boiled hamburger
- Popcorn
- Tortellini or other types of pasta (cooked)
- Bread (bagel pieces work great)
- Carrots
- Bananas
- Dried fruit
- Cheerios or other types of cereal
- Freeze-dried liver (found in pet stores and supply catalogs)
- Hot dogs (cooked)

To prevent your dog from getting diarrhea, don't give too much of any one thing. As your dog starts to like the training game, mix in less desirable treats (like dog food) with the yummy stuff so that he never knows what he's getting. Randomly reinforcing him with the higher-end treats will keep him more interested in the game, and let you accomplish more in each training session.

### Trick Tips: Tips on Treats

When it comes to rewards, people are often surprised to learn that dog cookies and dry dog food don't always cut it. Be creative with rewards—just be sure to keep the pieces tiny if you're using food. Even a Great Dane shouldn't get a treat larger than 1/4 inch. Using tiny treats will ensure that you'll be able to train for a longer period of time, because your dog won't get full too fast.

## Other Ideas for Rewards

Most of the time food rewards are used in training because they are quick and easy. But toys and games are an entirely different category of rewards that your dog might also find exciting. If your dog goes nuts over tennis balls or stuffed toys, or he likes Frisbees or chasing a flashlight beam, you can also use these as rewards, paired with the click.

### Trick Tips: Don't Over Treat

When you treat your dog with food, be sure you're not adding extra calories to his diet. You don't want to exceed his daily requirements. Whenever you've had an extra-long training session—and you've fed your dog extra treats—remember to cut back a bit on his daily ration of food.

For dogs who like games and toys, make your training sessions even more exciting by mixing them in with food rewards. Some sessions can be all food rewards, while others are all toys and games, or you can mix it up and see what elicits the best response. When using toys as a reward, the key is to make the play part brief and fun. The game might last five to ten seconds, and then the toy gets hidden and you get back to work. That way the reward doesn't distract the dog from the lesson. Here are some ideas for nonfood rewards:

- Playing a short game of fetch, tug-of-war, or catch
- Hiding a toy and finding it together
- Tossing a Frisbee
- Chasing a stream of bubbles
- Giving lots of happy praise and talk
- Petting your dog vigorously
- Playing flashlight tag (have your dog chase the light beam)
- Giving your dog a stuffed dog toy that makes noise or has a squeaker

Dogs are affectionate animals, and any time you spend praising them and showering them with attention is time well spent. Chances are, you'll get as much from the affection and exercise as they do!

## Help Your Dog Like Other Rewards

Some dogs love toys and will happily work for a toss of the ball—at least part of the time. But even dogs who aren't as crazy about toys can learn to like them if you work at it. It is worth the effort on your part to get your dog interested in varied rewards, because the more he finds rewarding the easier and more effective your training will be. Here's how to get started:

1. Hold your dog on a leash and tease him with a toy.
2. Throw the toy out of range then ignore his struggle toward it, but don't let him get it.
3. Use a helper to make the toy more exciting if necessary.
4. Wait patiently until the dog looks away from the toy and back at you.
5. Mark that moment with a click and allow him to play with the toy as the reward.
6. Back up slowly to increase the distance between the dog and the toy if he doesn't turn away from the toy in about thirty seconds. Click and release him to get the toy when your dog looks back at you.
7. Repeat this with different toys and allow the dog to go play with the helper every once in a while.
8. Keep the play part of the reward brief—about ten seconds.

Warming a dog up like this is a great way to start a training session—it helps the dog realize that it's time to work.

Exciting rewards are critical to an effective program. If your dog isn't turning himself inside out for the reward, find something he likes better. For dogs who have tons of toys but only play with a few, consider grouping them in sets of ten and rotating them each week to keep things interesting. But don't sweat it if you just can't get your dog interested in toys; remember, there's no crime in making your dog work for his food!

## Reward or Bribe?

Using food to teach your dog to perform tricks is simple, fun, and effective. However, many people complain that in the absence of food enticements their dog won't perform a behavior; this is because food is being used as a bribe. If food is used correctly, the dog should perform the behavior first, and then receive the reward. When food is used correctly, you won't need to use it to prompt your dog to do a trick. That's the critical difference between a reward and a bribe. A bribe is something that elicits a certain behavior by enticing the dog. A reward comes after the desired behavior has been performed.

Bribing can have its benefits, when you are in a hurry and out of options. If you are late for work and your dog is out in the yard and won't come in, you might shake a box of cookies to lure him inside. Your dog doesn't come when called under these circumstances and you are using the cookie promise to manage the situation. There isn't anything truly wrong with this, it does get the job done, but it isn't training and it will likely stop working after a while.

Trick Tips: Know the Difference

Being able to distinguish between bribes and rewards can mean the difference between a well-managed dog whose behavior is dependent upon your attentiveness and her hunger level, and the **well-trained** dog who responds to cues immediately and reliably because she knows that the consequences will be good.

A reward, on the other hand, occurs only after a behavior happens. A reward reinforces the likelihood that the behavior will happen again. For instance, you call your dog at the park and he comes to you; you offer a treat and release him back to play again. A rewarded dog is far more likely to come to you the next time you call than a dog who is just leashed and then put in the car to go home. There are two types of rewards at work here: the food reward, which reinforced the dog for coming back to his owner; and the consequence for coming back, which is the dog getting to go play again.

If you know your dog well—his energy level, personality, special talents, limitations, and motivations—you will be able to choose tricks that make both of you shine. Spend some time with your dog over the next few days and make notes on each of these categories. You may be surprised to learn how many things you assumed he would like that he actually doesn't. Adjusting your teaching style and training sessions can have a profound impact on the success of your training program.

## Providing the Right Foundation for Learning

Mental stimulation is an often-overlooked need in dogs. All dogs, regardless of breed or energy level, are intelligent and interactive creatures who love new experiences. Learning new things and solving problems makes life interesting and gives smart dogs something to do. It keeps them out of trouble, too!

Dogs who are tied outside, constantly frustrated, and emotionally neglected might start off friendly and welcoming, but eventually they become aggressive and wary of strangers. They have nothing to do, nothing to think about, no companionship, and are absolutely bored. Dogs like this, even early in their adult lives (two to three years old), are hard to train. It's a major effort to get them to sit, let alone perform more complex tricks. They aren't stupid or uncooperative, they're just blank. They simply do not know how to learn.

Lack of early stimulation and training makes it more difficult to teach any animal at a later date, because he has no basis for learning and doesn't quite know what to make of the attention. It is possible to teach these dogs, but it takes extra patience, repetition, and practice. The training techniques and tools described in subsequent chapters will help you teach your dog anything you care to take the time to teach.

### Trick Tips: Random Reinforcement

Once your dog starts mastering certain tricks, give him treats sporadically. He won't know for sure when he's getting a reward, but he probably won't take the chance on missing one, either.

## It's Never Too Soon to Start: Socializing Young Puppies

If you've just brought home a brand-new puppy, congratulations on this great addition to your family. Make sure you show him off—not for your sake, but for his. Begin teaching and socializing your puppy as early as eight weeks of age if he is properly vaccinated and your veterinarian has confirmed his good health. Socialization is an incredibly important process, and when it's neglected, puppies never reach their potential. They're less adaptable, harder to live with, and less happy. A dog who's received frequent and early socialization thrives on environment changes, interactions, and training procedures. He is also more likely to tolerate situations he's accidentally, and unfortunately, exposed to—such as kisses from a pushy visitor or a Big Wheel riding over his tail.

Start by providing a safe environment for your puppy to explore. No matter what you're socializing your puppy to, always approach it in a relaxed manner so he will learn to be comfortable and confident when encountering new things. Be sure to avoid any experiences that could be intimidating to a young pup, and remember to keep your dog leashed in unpredictable or potentially unsafe situations. This way, you can prevent a wobbly youngster from trying to pick him up, or keep him off the sidewalk as a skateboard zips by.

## Trick Tips: Don't Be Afraid to Try

You should never use any training method that makes you feel uncomfortable because you think it might hurt your dog. However, if you're positive a technique won't do any harm, but you're just not sure if it will work, go ahead and try it to see for yourself. Your dog will benefit greatly from having an owner who is not afraid to try new techniques and is committed to finding the best way possible to train him to be the best companion he can be.

## Teach Your Dog to Think

Using the methods in this book will teach your dog how to think and solve problems, which is important for any dog. The techniques are commonly referred to as "clicker training," and are based in proven scientific theory. The rules and guidelines (see Chapter 3) will show you how to use this method to teach your dog anything physically possible. It is so exciting to see a dog grasp the concept of what you are trying to accomplish, and respond well without needing any corrections!

All puppies should attend a well-run puppy kindergarten class that teaches basic commands (Sit, Down, Stay, Come), how to walk without pulling, and how to come when called. The class should also offer a playtime for dogs in the eight- to eighteen-week range, and should be staff-supervised so everyone has a good experience. It is crucial to the normal social development of your dog that she gets to play with other puppies and safe, well-socialized adult dogs on a regular basis. The more good experiences your young puppy has the easier it will be to teach her anything later in life.

Here's a list of qualities to look for in your dog-training school:

- A limited class size with an instructor/assistant-to-student ratio of 1:6 is ideal.
- The age range of the puppies accepted should be no older than eighteen weeks.

- Handouts or homework sheets to explain exercises are important so that lessons can be shared among family members.
- The whole family should be welcome to attend. (If you include your children, make sure you bring along another adult to supervise them while you focus on training the dog.)
- All training methods should be positively based and use clicker training, ideally.
- Demonstrations should be given with untrained dogs to show the progression of exercises.
- Volunteers or assistants who help with the management of the class should be available to ensure that you get the help you need.

Especially if you find it difficult to block out specific time for training, enrolling in a group class will motivate you to practice consistently with your dog. In addition to obedience classes, many schools also offer agility classes, tricks classes, flyball, tracking, hunting, herding, and other types of dog sports, so once your dog has mastered the basics, you'll have plenty of opportunities to move on to more advanced trick training.

## Trick Tips: Relationship Building

As you read and do research you will find that there is no one way to train a dog. You are your dog's primary caretaker, and it's your job to find the methods that get the job done without harming your relationship. Find a trainer who emphasizes building your relationship with your dog.

Learning something new is more fun when you have the right tools and support—so be sure that the training school's philosophy matches your own and that you feel comfortable there. The best judge of a good puppy kindergarten, or any obedience class for that matter, is you. Ask if you can observe a class before signing up your puppy. Make sure the methods taught are kind and gentle, and that the puppies seem to be getting it. Go on your gut instinct—if you like the instructor and she seems like a person you can learn from, sign up. Train your dog; it's the nicest way to say you love him!

## Quick Fix: Work in a Group

Taking a group obedience class can be especially great for dogs who have trouble concentrating on training. The distraction of other dogs will help your dog to realize that she must learn to pay close attention to you. Make sure the ratio of teachers to students is high in your class; twelve students to two instructors is ideal.

### Practice Makes Perfect

As with anything in which you want to excel, the more you practice the better at it you will become. All training is a learned skill; the more you work with your dog, the more effective you'll be as a trainer and as a team. For example, the beginning trainer's timing often needs some work. Through lots of practice, you will find and develop your own training style, discovering what works for you and expanding upon it.

There are tons of books and online resources that will tell you everything you'll ever want to know about dog behavior and training. Search for obedience classes in your area and keep at it. Remember that you and your dog are going to be together for a long time—if you're lucky maybe even ten to twelve years or longer. Time spent teaching her how to learn will benefit both of you for years to come. Start your dog on the road to higher learning today!

### Getting Your Dog Moving

As mentioned earlier in this chapter, adequate exercise is essential for dogs. Exercise is a crucial element in any training program, and without enough of it, no real learning will occur. A dog without enough exercise is like a child without recess. What adult would like to teach a math lesson to a classroom full of six-year-old boys who haven't been

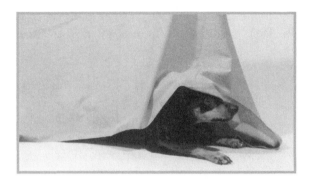

Miniature Pinscher "peeking" out from under a blanket

outside to play all day? Without exercise, your dog will be hard to teach because he just can't be still long enough to pay attention.

Dogs vary in their exercise requirements, but all need at least thirty to sixty minutes of running, playing, and interaction with you or other dogs each day. The amount and type of exercise is dependent upon your dog's overall energy level. A Border Collie or energetic young Lab will need one to two hours of flat-out running and active play, while a couch potato Pekingese might only need a thirty-minute romp. Yet, every dog is different, regardless of the breed and its stereotype. Ultimately, the proper amount of exercise is whatever it takes to make your dog tired enough to be able to exist in your home as a calm, relaxed member of the family. Following are some clues that your dog isn't getting enough exercise:

- She paces from room to room in the house.
- She hardly ever lies down, even when everyone else is relaxed.
- She whines excessively for no apparent reason.
- She barks excessively, sometimes over nothing.
- She digs, destroys, and chews everything in sight.
- She never stops jumping when there are people around.
- She runs away every chance she gets.
- She runs along the fence to bark at passersby.

If your dog exhibits some or all of these symptoms, she could probably use more exercise and mental stimulation. Most people don't realize that leaving their dogs in the backyard for hours at a time is not a good way for dogs to burn off energy and not nearly enough exercise to relax them. Most dogs, when left to their own devices, don't do anything but bark, dig, or lay around.

### Quick Fix: Exercise Enhances Training

Energetic dogs who don't get enough exercise are easy to spot: They demonstrate their excess energy through barking, jumping, and other unwanted behavior. If your dog has behavior problems, increasing the amount of exercise he gets can cut your training time in half.

If you're going to use your yard as a way to exercise your dog, you will need to go out with her and play games to burn off even a tenth of the energy she's got bottled up. In case you don't have a lot of time during the day to play with your pup, sign up for doggie day care, or hire a pet sitter to exercise your dog while you're at work so that when you come home you can concentrate on training your dog and have a willing student who is ready to work. Inviting neighbor dogs over to play, if your dog gets along with them, might be another option. Any way you look at it, all-out running, chasing, and wrestling is what a dog needs to do in order to be tired enough to be a good pet.

## Working out Together

For dog owners with an active lifestyle, there are lots of ways a healthy, lively dog can burn off energy while accompanying you. Jogging, mountain biking, and Rollerblading are excellent ways to exercise dogs with boundless energy. Just make sure that you start off slowly and gradually build the distance. Also, pay attention to your dog's feet, checking them frequently for cuts and scrapes. Try to have him run on a variety of surfaces, since pavement is hard on a dog's joints and bones.

Dogs who participate in such activities should be at least one year old and recently checked by their veterinarian for potential health problems. (Just like with people, vigorous exercise can exacerbate certain bone and joint disorders.) A fit dog is happy, focused, and more likely to participate in activities for longer periods of time and without injury.

## Dog Sports and Activities

The reason we get a dog in the first place is to enjoy their company and share them with other people. Depending on your dog's personality and activity level, you may consider participating with your dog in any of a great variety of dog sports or activities. Enrolling your dog in an agility class might be an excellent way to introduce both of you to something new while maintaining a good level of fitness. Agility is an obstacle course for dogs involving things to climb over, around, and through, as well as hurdles to jump over. The course is timed and dependent on you being able to successfully lead your dog through a maze of obstacles to the finish. (For more on agility training, see Chapter 11.)

### Quick Fix: Seek Additional Exercise Options

In this dog-friendly age of ours, services like doggie day care, play groups, and dog parks are available to help us exercise our restless pooches. If you try to fit in more exercise sessions, but just can't seem to put a dent in your dog's energy, consider doggie day care one or two days a week.

If you would like to be an active participant in your dog's exercise program, you will find that there are many canine sports that require you to be almost as fit as your dog. From flyball to tracking to search and rescue, the possibilities are endless. If your style is quieter, you may consider a visiting-therapy dog program that allows you to go and visit a hospital or nursing home on a weekly or monthly basis. This is an excellent way to meet other dog owners and keep your dog's obedience skills sharp, because you will be using them constantly.

If you have a lot of free time and financial resources, you also may consider becoming part of the growing search and rescue dog teams that look for missing people locally and nationally. No matter what your interest, there is a dog sport out there that you and your pup will both enjoy.

### Games Dogs Play

Games are a great way to boost your dog's interest in learning new things and strengthen your bond with him at the same time. Keep the rules simple and easy to follow, and play often. Involve as many people in the family as you can, and see how much you'll enjoy learning new ways of interacting together. Consider any of the following activities and games:

- Play fetch—a great way to tire out a tireless retriever. Use a tennis racquet to hit the ball even farther for all-out sprints.
- Go swimming—another excellent activity for a very active dog. Combine it with some retrieving for a really exhausting workout.
- Play hide-and-seek—an indoor rainy-day game might provide some dogs with enough activity to relax them for the rest of the day. Also use this game to perk up your dog's recall and teach him that coming to you is always the best option.
- Hide your dog's toys—he'll learn to use his nose to track things down *and* bring them back to you.
- Exercise the brain—set up a treat-dispensing toy, and show your dog how to interact with it until it pays off.

Whatever game you play, be sure to have a blast with your dog! Keep the pace fast and interesting, and you will see your dog perk up at the mere mention of playtime with you.

## Don't Forget Safety!

Keep your dog's safety in mind while you are training, and pay attention to her physical limitations. If you have a long-backed breed like a basset hound for instance, it may not be a good idea to teach her to Sit Up Pretty, since her torso would be awfully heavy to support on such short legs. For larger breeds like Great Danes and Saint Bernards, you may not want to do any tricks that involve jumping, since the impact of landing is not good for their joints.

### Trick Tips: Watch for Injuries

If your dog refuses to assume a certain position when you're training, don't be afraid to have her checked for an injury. Dogs are stoic animals and rarely show discomfort unless it's obvious. Hiding injuries is instinctive, stemming from their wolf cousins who live by the rule of survival of the fittest.

Also pay attention to your dog's weight, since extra pounds can lead to injuries. If you respect your dog's physical limitations, he will amaze you with his willingness to try what you ask. A dog cannot tell you outright if something is uncomfortable, so do your best to read his body language and go slowly. As often as possible, perform on a soft surface like a rug, grass, or sand, especially for tricks involving jumping, spinning, or rolling. Being mindful of your environment will minimize injuries and make your dog more comfortable when doing tricks.

## Make the Most of Special Talents and Interests

Depending on a dog's breed characteristics, he will often display a natural talent for certain tricks. For instance, Labrador and Golden Retrievers often excel at tricks that involve having things in their mouths, like Put Away Your Toys or Go Fetch Me a Coke from the

Refrigerator. Herding breeds might prefer to learn directional tricks like spinning to the left or right. Likewise, a small dog who stands on her hind legs a lot may be a great candidate to learn Sit Up and Beg or Dance, while a large-breed dog may be perfect for Play Dead, especially if he is of the low-energy mindset.

The most important thing to remember here is that any dog can master tricks that are physically possible for her to do. Dogs are amazing creatures, and they are so willing to be with us and please us that they will put up with a lot, just as long as they are getting some attention. With enough patience and practice, and the right training tools, you can teach your dog to do just about any trick you like!

## Chapter 3

# Positive Reinforcement, Not Punishment

Training your dog to behave properly is integral before any sort of more advanced trick training can occur. Obedience training is an ongoing process that constantly requires you to prevent, interrupt, and redirect your dog's less-than-stellar behavior. As humans, we are absolutely convinced that in order to change behavior we must provide some sort of punishment that will eliminate bad habits altogether. In truth, no animals, including humans, respond well to punishment. Although it has been part of training dogs for decades, punishment is not a good or effective way to train a well-behaved family pet.

## The Problem with Punishment

Over time, many trainers have found that it is totally unnecessary to use punishment to prompt reliable, acceptable behavior. In many cases, using punishment can actually make some problems worse. Consider these two points:

- Punishment stops behavior, but it does not teach or provide another choice.
- The many negative side effects of punishment outweigh the short-term benefits.

The best human example of why punishment is ineffective is a speeding ticket. If you've ever been pulled over for speeding, you'll understand. The moment when the lights flash behind you is horrible. When you're actually pulled over, your heart races, you stutter and stammer, and then you wait and wait and wait for the police officer to deliver the ticket. Now you've got a fine to pay, and points on your insurance as well. Do you stop speeding? For a little while you might, but just wait until the next day you find yourself running late—you're back to speeding again, and you get away with it.

You were probably a little more careful this next time, avoiding speed traps and keeping your eyes open, but you were speeding. After being punished severely only weeks before, how could you go back to that behavior? Quite simply, the punishment made you a better speeder! You are no longer a random, careless speeder; you actually look for cruisers and avoid known speed traps. The punishment actually improved the way you speed.

### Punishment Is Reactive

The first problem with punishment is that it is a response to bad behavior, whereas training initiates good behavior. The second problem with punishment as a training tool is that you can't always control what the student learns. Punishment is not effective for fixing behavior problems because it is only part of the equation. It stops the unwanted behavior, but it does not show the dog what he should have done instead. Plus, by the time punishment is delivered it is too late to teach the dog anything, because he has already done something undesirable, and it can't be undone.

Punishing your dog for jumping on the company will not make him want to sit in front of them next time. In fact, punishment delivered by a visitor or in the presence of one might actually teach your dog to be fearful of visitors because it's sometimes unpleasant to be around them. This is not what you want to teach your dog. After all the work you put into encouraging your dog to be social around people, punishing him for being friendly could be detrimental.

### Timing Is Everything

For punishment to mean anything, the timing of the correction has to be precise; it must happen the moment the undesirable behavior begins. Not many people, especially average pet owners, are capable of doing this. But even if you were able to respond immediately, usually at the time of the correction the dog is overstimulated and excited, which means her brain is not in learning mode. In order to process information a dog has to be in a fairly relaxed state.

If the timing of the correction were perfect, the dog would need to be rewarded as soon as the inappropriate behavior stopped, because the timing of the reward is the instructive part for the dog. When trying to fix a behavior the dog has been practicing for a long time, a very high rate of reinforcement for the right behavior must be employed. Otherwise, the new, desirable behavior will not replace the old behavior. Remember that old habits die hard, and it is difficult to adopt new ways of doing things without being heavily reinforced for the right choices.

## Redirecting the Behavior

Instead of using corrections, at the first sign of alert or tension, either interrupt the dog or redirect his attention in an appropriate manner.

You can say the dog's name, touch the dog on the shoulder, or turn away from whatever captured the dog's interest.

To work effectively, interruptions must be delivered before the dog starts the behavior. In the case of barking, for instance, if you wait until the dog is loud and frantic you will not be able to distract him from what he's barking at in order to teach him anything. Even a strong correction wouldn't phase some one-track-minded dogs. This is like trying to reason with a person who is angry. When someone is in an irrational frame of mind, they just aren't capable of listening or being reasonable.

Instead, start paying attention to what triggers the barking, and interrupt the dog while he's still thinking about it. To short-circuit an undesirable behavior, you might have the dog go to his bed, or move further away from the distractions so he's not as excited. Eventually, your goal is to interrupt him close to the distractions in the environments where the undesirable behavior occurs, but it is unreasonable to try to train him there in the beginning. As with any constructive and lasting training, you need to start with small, simple steps that enable the dog to be successful.

### Trick Tips: Dealing with Distractions

Repeating a command when a dog is obviously too distracted to hear what you are saying is not teaching the dog anything but how to ignore you. Help the dog perform the behavior with a treat or toy as a lure. Drill the dog for five to ten repetitions to get him working again, and then wean him off the extra help. With patience and practice, it won't be long before your dog understands that his training works everywhere, regardless of the distraction.

## Establishing New Patterns

In order to stop unwanted behavior and teach your dog new habits, you must have a set plan to accomplish your goal, and you must prevent the dog from practicing the old behavior while you are retraining her. Setting up a new pattern of behavior isn't easy for dogs, because they get into habits like we do and tend to do things the same way again and again if we let them.

## Repetition

The important thing to remember when changing a pattern is that you need to practice the new pattern over and over and reward the dog repeatedly for the new behavior until she adopts it as her own. In the meantime, if you want to get where you are going faster, you need to stop allowing the dog to reinforce herself for the wrong behavior by preventing it from happening. Stepping on the leash to prevent jumping will not, by itself, teach your dog to sit, but it will reduce her options and make sitting more likely, because that is the only behavior getting rewarded.

## An Ounce of Prevention

The more time you spend with dogs, the more you will find that management is a large part of training. Gates, crates, and pens can be your best friends when raising and training a dog. Although they don't teach the dog not to chew the couch or pee on the carpet, they prevent inappropriate behaviors from becoming bad habits. Managing a dog's environment helps him to do the right things by limiting his choices. Preventing your dog from repeating negative patterns isn't the solution to all of your behavior problems, but it is integral.

For example, a fence is a management tool for dogs who enjoy playing in their yards and owners who want to keep them there. A baby gate in the kitchen limits the dog's freedom so that he can't get into trouble in the rest of the house while you're not around. And when you don't have time to teach your dog to sit for a guest, it's better to gate him off than allow him to dive on the visitor or bolt out the front door.

## The Fallout of Punishment: Aggression

Punishment that is mistimed or severe can often cause serious problems. Dogs don't learn to like people or other dogs when they are corrected for barking and lunging. In fact, many of these animals become more unpredictable and aggressive, because they learn that the presence of other dogs or people means they are about to get punished.

Growling is a dog's way of warning us that he is uncomfortable and that there will be trouble if the bothersome person or dog doesn't go away. If you physically punish a dog for growling he might stop growling, but you could make him far more dangerous. Instead of warning people when he is distressed, he could just skip straight to the bite instead. You have, in essence, created a better biter. Punishing the warning doesn't make sense; we want to change the way the dog feels about the person or dog, not take away the warning that he is about to bite. Growling lets us know we have a problem and gives us time to do something about it—like teach the dog a positive association with people and dogs—before the dog bites.

## Training versus Punishment

Never use punishment with any problem related to aggression around people or dogs—the risk of creating a better biter is just too high. Here are five reasons to teach your dog instead of punish him.

1. Punishment must be repeated frequently to remind the dog to avoid her mistake.
2. Punishment doesn't teach the dog anything; dogs with little confidence will wilt.
3. With punishment, you can't control what the dog learns.
4. Punishment can damage the relationship between owner and dog.
5. Punishment can accelerate aggression by suppressing all precursors to aggression, so the dog skips right to the bite.

There are many reasons not to use punishment, but in general, punishment misses the point and won't get you where you want to go. It comes too late to be instructive and has the danger of teaching the dog to be better at the very behavior you are trying to eliminate.

If you think you need to use punishment, it is probably an indicator of a much larger issue. Most likely the real problem is that your dog needs more information about what she has to do to be right. Instead of spending your time figuring out how to stop the behaviors you don't like, map out what you do want your dog to do and retrain her.

## The Kindness Revolution in Dog Training

It's clear that old methods of training—making the dog "obey"—not only are outdated, but also do not evolve your dog's problem-solving skills or intelligence. These days, it is easier to avoid using punishment because better alternatives are available. It isn't necessary to use brute force or intimidation to make a dog comply; through use of a clicker and treats, dog training has become kinder and gentler to both the dog and the owner. Clicker training isn't a gimmick or the latest fad; it is a scientifically based technique that uses the principles of operant conditioning. It's an intelligent, timesaving endeavor that promotes positive reinforcement through the use of treats and a clicker in order to teach your dog to think.

Training your dog with treats and a clicker is the fastest, most reliable way to teach your dog what you expect of him and have fun while you are doing it. There is no need to coerce, push, or shove to get what you want; once your dog knows how to learn, you will have a willing partner and a better overall relationship. Many families who have learned to train their dogs with a clicker and treats have enjoyed the learning process so much that they have come back again and again for more advanced classes.

The application of clicker training to dogs is pure genius; it simplifies and speeds up the process of learning for dogs and owners alike. Handlers of any age or size can learn the principles of clicker training, and since it is not dependent on corrections or physical manipulation, the size, strength, and stamina of the handler doesn't matter.

## Using the Clicker

The clicker is a small plastic box with a metal tab that makes a clicking sound when you push down with your thumb. When the box is clicked the dog gets a treat, and after a few repetitions the dog learns to associate the sound of the clicker with a food reward. It's easy to find clickers at larger chain pet stores, or you can order them from dog training Web sites, such as *www.clickertraining.com*.

Golden Retriever
holding keys

### Why It Works

Pairing the clicker with a food reward is a powerful way to communicate to our dogs about which behaviors are rewardable. Rather than helping your dog or physically manipulating his body, you teach your dog to learn by trial and error. Because the click noticeably marks the desired action, the dog is able to identify specifically which behavior earned the reward (this is especially handy with a very active dog). The power of clicker training lies in the click; the sound of the click means that a reward is coming and allows you to give feedback to the dog by marking the exact moment he does the correct behavior.

Think of the click as a snapshot of what the dog is doing at the exact moment he is doing it. Marking this moment with the click makes it easier for the dog to understand what he has done to get his reward. Training your dog in this way will get him excited about the learning process since it gives him the responsibility of making the click happen.

### The Clicker as an Event Marker

Part of the reason why using a clicker is so integral to successful training is because the sound of the click is unique and like nothing else the dog has ever heard. People often ask about using their voice instead of the clicker to mark appropriate behavior, but in the initial stages of training your voice is not a good event marker. Since you talk to your dog all the time, your voice does not have the same startling effect that the clicker has. Because the clicker's unique sound reaches the part of the brain that is also responsible for the fight-or-flight response, it really captures the dog's attention.

## Shaping

Clicker training is all about the process of shaping behavior, which means breaking it down into steps that progress toward an end goal. Shaping is not a rigid list of steps, but rather a general guide to get from point A to point B with lots of room for variation, intuition, rapid progress (skipping steps), or reviewing if the steps are too big.

There are two types of shaping. Prompted shaping uses a food lure or target to elicit desired behaviors; free shaping requires you to wait for the dog to offer desired actions on his own, then reward him with a treat in order to capture the small steps that lead toward the end goal.

For behaviors that involve natural talents or unusual behaviors, free shaping is the way to go. With free shaping, the dog is fully in charge of which behaviors he is offering, so he will often learn faster (in some situations) and retain more than when you prompt his behavior with a lure or target. Keep in mind, however, that free shaping can be time consuming, since it depends upon the dog offering behavior, and this requires patience on the handler's part.

Whichever type of shaping you use, remember, you'll reach your goals faster if you have a plan, so keep notes on what you teach. Notice whether your dog catches on to the components as presented, or if she needs more explicit direction. Detailed notes make it easy to pick up where you left off, and your training sessions will be more productive overall.

## Using Lures

A lure is a piece of food used to elicit behavior. Its goal is to help the dog get into the right position in order to earn the click and treat. It's sometimes frustrating and time consuming for a beginning dog trainer to wait for the dog to offer the right behavior, so food lures often get things going more quickly. The problem with food lures, however, is that unless they are faded relatively quickly, the dog (and humans) become dependent on them. If you continue to rely on food lures, you won't ever have a well-trained dog who obeys on cue; all you'll have is a dog who follows food.

As a general rule, help the dog into position and lure her six times in a row. On the seventh repetition, do all the same motions with your body, but without the food lure in your hand. You can start fading the lure gradually by putting it on a nearby table and running to get it after the click. This way, the dog knows it's there and is excited about it but is not dependent on you waving it around to get her into the right position. Then, if the dog performs the behavior correctly, click and treat. If she doesn't perform the behavior correctly, go back and lure her six more times and try it again.

### Quick Fix: To Lure or Not to Lure?

For some dogs, lures are a great tool for prompting behavior. For others, however, lures present more of a distraction and hindrance than help. If this is true for your dog, you should skip lures altogether.

These mini drilling sessions train the dog to perform the correct behavior and show you if she understands what has prompted the click. This will help your dog to learn that she is working for the click, and that the treat is an afterthought.

## Targeting

Targeting is a form of luring, but it removes the treat by a step by teaching the dog to touch his nose to an object. This tool can be used to move your dog or to have him interact with someone or something. Any item can be used, but the three main targets are your hand, a lid to a yogurt container, and a target stick. (You can buy a target stick online at *www.clickertraining.com* or make your own out of a short piece of dowel.) Keep in mind that the same rules apply regarding weaning dogs off of targets: Use targets to get the behavior started, and then slowly phase it out.

## Hand Target

To teach your dog to target your hand with his nose follow these steps:

1. Hold your hand palm-up with a piece of food tucked under your thumb in the center of your palm. Click and treat your dog for sniffing your hand.
2. Keep the food in your hand for six repetitions and then take the food out and repeat, clicking the dog for touching his nose to your palm.
3. Have the dog follow your hand in all directions while you move around the room.
4. Involve a helper and have your dog target your hand and then your helper's hand for clicks and treats.
5. Label the behavior of touching his nose to your hand by saying "Touch" right before the dog's nose hits your hand. (More on labeling follows.)
6. Try the trick in new places and with new people until your dog is fluent. Don't be afraid to go back to using food for a few repetitions if your dog falls apart around a new distraction.

## Lid Target

On occasion, you might want your dog to move away from you to perform a behavior at a distance. In that case, it might be useful for you to teach your dog to target a yogurt lid with her nose. The steps for teaching your dog to target a lid are:

1. Put the lid in your hand and hold a treat in the center with your thumb.
2. When your dog noses at it, click and treat. Repeat six times.
3. Present the lid with no treat and click and treat for sniffing or nose bumping.

4. Label the behavior by saying "Touch" again just before your dog touches the lid.

5. Put the lid on the floor close by and repeat, clicking your dog at first for moving toward the lid and then for actually touching it with her nose.

6. Move the lid at varying distances until you can send her across the room to bump it with her nose for a click and treat.

### Quick Fix: The Two-in-a-Row Rule

When training, try not to let your dog be wrong more than twice before helping him into the correct position, lessening the distraction, or changing the variables. If your dog makes more than two mistakes in a row, you need to change something so that he can be right more easily.

### Stick Target

The target stick acts like an extension of your arm and is useful when working with your dog at a short distance. The steps for teaching your dog to touch a target stick with his nose are as follows:

1. Put the end of the stick in the palm of your hand with a treat and click and treat your dog for sniffing or nudging it with his nose.

2. Gradually work your hand up the stick and only click and treat your dog for touching his nose close to the end away from your hand.

3. Try putting the stick on the floor and only clicking and treating when your dog touches the ends.

4. Have your dog follow the stick as you walk with him until he's racing to catch the end of it for a click and treat.

### Paw Targeting

There are times when you might want your dog to use her paw to interact with an object. The difference between teaching your dog to target with her paw instead of her nose involves paying attention to which body part is hitting the target.

1. Put your hand or lid out for the dog to see, but withhold the click until she steps near it. Because you have already taught your dog to target with her nose, she might offer only this behavior at first. Be patient and wait for paw action near the target.
2. Withhold the click to let your dog know that you want something other than a nose touch and see what happens.
3. Make it easy on your dog by moving the lid or your hand along the floor so that you can click her for moving toward it. An easy way to help your dog to get this behavior started is to put the lid at the base of the stairs and click her for stepping on or next to it.
4. When you withhold the click your dog might get frustrated, but don't be too quick to help right away; wait and see if she'll paw at the target or move toward it.
5. Practice a paw target separately from a nose target and be sure to have two distinct cues for each one.
6. Keep in mind that short, frequent training sessions will help your dog figure out what you want faster than long, confusing ones.

For targeting to be useful, you must practice it often. The more experience your dog has with this method, the better it will serve you in your training.

## Labeling Behavior

The major difference between clicker training and other types of training is that you don't label behaviors right away, because early versions are not what you want as the final result. A label can be a verbal cue, a hand signal, or both, but it should not be introduced until the dog offers a decent version of it. If you label behavior too soon you will get a wide variety of responses from the dog. But if you reserve the label until the behavior looks close to perfect, then you will be sure that the dog has properly connected what is being clicked.

**Quick Fix: On Cue**

To replace an old cue with a new one, you need to present the new cue immediately before the old, exaggerated cue. Gradually make the exaggerated cue less exaggerated until the new cue prompts the behavior to occur.

You can call each behavior anything you want; just make it a simple one-syllable word as often as possible, and be sure it doesn't sound too much like any other word you use with your dog. Dogs pick up a lot from your body language and the pitch of your voice, but they sometimes have trouble distinguishing between similar sounding words, such as *no* and *go*, for instance.

## Weaning off the Clicker and Treats

Once your dog is reliably performing a behavior on cue (with 100 percent accuracy), he is ready to be weaned off the clicker and treats. (Remember: The click and treat always go together; don't click without treating because the value of the reward marker, the click, will become diluted and less meaningful to the dog.) The worst thing you can do when you are weaning your dog off the clicker and treats is to do it cold turkey, because it's too abrupt and frustrates the dog. Instead, wean gradually, by having your dog repeat a behavior more than once before you click and treat. This shows the dog that he must continue to perform the behavior until he hears his click.

**Quick Fix: Count Your Calories**

Don't use too many dog biscuits when treating your pup. Dog biscuits can be very fattening—when it comes to calories, one cookie is like eating a snack-size candy bar. Instead, use very tiny pieces of unique foods your dog really likes, like cheese, chicken, or soft dog treats.

The key to weaning is going slowly, getting the dog to perform longer versions of the behavior, or performing it in more repetitions successfully. The weaning process might be a good time to start introducing nonfood rewards, such as the opportunity to greet a guest after sitting, or being released to go play with other dogs after coming when called. However you do it, weaning your dog off lots of extra commands and prompting accompanied by food lures will make you both relaxed in public, because you know what to expect from each other.

## A Word on Food

Clicker training is successful because the emphasis is on the click, not the treat. Once dogs figure out the game, they love it and will gladly work regardless of how they feel about food. If you have a finicky fellow, try diversifying what you use as the reward and cutting back a little on his daily meal. For dogs who like to eat: Clicker training uses a lot of food rewards, but that doesn't mean you'll have a fat dog. Remember, the size of the rewards should be tiny—¼ of an inch or less—and can even be drawn from the dog's meals. The length of your sessions should be five to ten minutes maximum, so your dog is not going to be getting a lot of extra treats at one time. If your dog is on a special diet, consult your veterinarian about what food treats you can use.

The beauty of clicker training is that it teaches dogs to think. It is a kind, nonviolent way to teach a dog what is expected of her. It is also long-lasting and easy, making it enjoyable for the trainer and trainee alike. Once you and your dog get the hang of it, you can use clicker training to teach your dog anything your heart desires, including some of the coolest tricks around!

## Chapter 4

# Solving Problems

By now you know that punishment is not the solution to your dog's problems, and you have an idea of some good alternatives for breaking inappropriate behaviors. Still, that recognition probably doesn't help a whole lot when you're eager to teach your pooch some fun tricks, yet you can't even stop her from whining, nipping, and barking. You need only visit an animal shelter to see how many dogs between the age of nine months and two years have been left homeless, after their families simply gave up when they couldn't deal with their pup's antics. This sad situation is completely avoidable, however. Most families throw in the towel because they think their dog's behavior is so problematic it can't be fixed. In truth, it's usually because they didn't put forth the time, energy, or dedication to socializing and training their dogs properly.

The root of many dogs' behavior problems lies in a lack of stimulation and energy outlets. Dogs are pack animals who are meant to live in groups; they are not solitary animals and do not enjoy spending hours alone for days at a time. Behavior problems don't have to lead to the dog being left at an animal shelter—you just need to understand how dogs think and what motivates them to do what they do.

When you take a dog into your home, you must make room for her. Dogs require a lot of love and training and care, but they give so much more back in loyalty and love. Be sure to give her the best home you possibly can—you will be rewarded a hundred fold. If your dog's behavior is less than ideal, don't give up on her. Remember that all dogs, no matter how sweet and compliant they are, need training, limits, exercise, and house rules. Set those things straight first, and soon enough you'll move on to teaching fun, enjoyable tricks.

## Analyze the Problem

When it comes to solving their dog's behavior problems, people often think too much. For instance, they blame the dog for messing on the carpet out of spite when in reality the dog isn't being walked enough! Let's be clear here: Dogs don't hold grudges, and they don't do things out of spite. Dogs are not capable of those thoughts. They live in the moment, they are opportunistic, and they repeat behavior that is rewarded, even if it's rewarded negatively.

Trick Tips: The Power of Positive Reinforcement

For decades, animals in zoos, aquariums, and circuses have been trained using positive reinforcement. Can you imagine putting a training collar on a killer whale to try to make him jump? The same principle applies to dogs. Just because you **can** force dogs to obey doesn't mean you **should**. Don't force your dog to do anything—teach him to think instead!

Dogs are animals, and animals do things that sometimes baffle humans, despite our best attempts to understand them. In order to solve an existing behavior problem, it is crucial to sit down with your family members and figure out the details of the problem. Using the following questions as a guide, try to identify and define what the dog is actually doing, when he is doing it, and what you might be able to teach him to do instead.

- Identify the problem. What does the dog actually do? Write it down and describe it in as much detail as possible.
- Understand the cause. What triggers the dog's behavior? Is it the presence of a strange dog, the doorbell, or a new person?
- Think about frequency. How often does the dog do the behavior? Only once in a while, or nonstop? Every time the trigger is present, or only half the time?
- Consider the consequence. What has been done to stop the behavior? What consequence results when the dog responds to the trigger?
- Recognize reinforcement history. How long has the dog been behaving this way, and what is reinforcing him to repeat the pattern?
- Manage the problem. What can you do to prevent the dog from continuing the behavior while you are retraining him?

By identifying the actual source of the problem, you will be able to develop a plan for retraining your dog to respond in a more appropriate way. Let everyone who takes care of the dog participate in the exercise, as well as future training sessions.

## Behavior Management

Prevention isn't training, but it can help you get rid of unwanted behavior, because you are not allowing the dog to practice it repeatedly. "Management" involves putting the dog in a separate room or crate when visitors arrive or stepping on the leash to prevent the dog from jumping. The less the dog gets to practice the wrong behavior, the less you will have to do to convince him that the right behavior is more rewarding and desirable. Behavior management does *not* mean correcting, reprimanding, or punishing your dog.

Some people manage their dog's behavior with crates, gates, and pens; others use leashes or time outs. It doesn't matter how you manage your dog's behavior, as long as it keeps your dog from practicing the wrong behavior over and over. Consider these behavior management ideas:

- Use a crate when you can't watch your dog if he is a destructive chewer.
- Keep a leash on your dog when company visits, and put your foot on it to prevent jumping.
- Don't allow your dog off leash in public places if he doesn't come when he's called.
- Avoid other dogs if your dog is aggressive around them.
- If your dog likes to escape out the front door, deny access to it.
- If your dog likes to bite the mailman, don't tie him outside the front door.
- If your dog is not fully housebroken, don't allow him unsupervised freedom.

Use management and prevention tactics to keep a behavior problem from perpetuating itself while you are retraining your dog to do something more appropriate. Prevention is not a 100-percent solution, but it can help you move toward your goal by not reinforcing inappropriate behavior.

## Encouraging Alternate Behavior

Okay. You've gotten to the root of your dog's less-than-desirable behavior, and you have an interim plan in place—management. The next step is understanding reinforcement and replacement behavior. You need to provide reinforcement for a behavior other than the one you don't like. Otherwise, the dog will revert back to the old behavior. Think about reinforcing a behavior that is easy to teach and easy for the dog to perform, even with a lot of distractions.

### Trick Tips: Shape Up!

Free shaping is definitely worth adding to your bag of training tricks. It helps to give you lots of options in explaining what you want your dog to do. You just show up with your clicker and treats, then click and treat what you like and ignore what you don't.

### Recognizing Self-Rewarding Behavior

First off, look closely at the circumstances surrounding the misbehavior and see what your dog finds reinforcing about it. If he jumps and people yell at him and shove him off, perhaps he likes the attention and they should ignore him instead. Or maybe there is a member of your household who encourages the dog to jump and isn't consistent about reinforcing the dog for sitting instead.

By removing the source of the reinforcement, you can put a good dent in getting rid of a behavior problem. In many cases the dog is getting way too much response for the wrong behavior and needs more information about what is going right. If there isn't anything going right, then the dog has too much freedom and too many options. In this case, you'll need to rethink your training program and make it easier for your dog to be right.

### Reinforcing the Right Behavior

To change a behavior that has become a habit, you need to provide a high rate of reinforcement for the appropriate behavior or it will never occur to the dog to try anything else. Dogs do what works, so if they get attention for the wrong behavior, they are likely to repeat it in the future. But if they are reinforced for a more appropriate behavior with really yummy treats or exciting games of fetch, they will make those good things happen again by repeating the behavior.

Every reinforcement for the right behavior is like money in the bank. If your dog's bank account for undesirable behavior is high, you will need to build up a considerable reinforcement history for the alternate behavior. Practice often, give occasional jackpots (a handful of small goodies or an extra-long game of fetch or tug), and set your dog up to succeed.

### Training an Incompatible Behavior

Every time a dog practices an old, undesirable action, he builds up his bank account of negative behavior, so it's crucial to replace it with a more appropriate option. Make sure that the new behavior you teach instead is incompatible with the undesirable behavior. Teaching an acceptable replacement behavior solves many problems because a dog can't do two things at once. There's no way, for instance, for a dog to jump on a stranger if she's taught to sit politely when greeting a person. So if you reinforce sitting as the desirable behavior when your dog greets new people, eventually she won't even try to jump. Teaching your dog an alternate behavior gives you more control over her, and it also allows you to reward her for an appropriate response. Perhaps your dog could:

- Greet visitors with a toy in her mouth instead of jumping on them.
- Go to her bed or mat when the doorbell rings.
- Retrieve a toy instead of barking out the window at passersby.
- Look at you instead of lunging at other dogs.
- Target your hand (see Chapter 3) instead of running away.
- Do a play bow when she sees another dog.

Use this opportunity to be creative, and find solutions that suit your needs and your dog's natural inclinations. Think of this as another way you're making it easy for training to be successful.

Be forewarned: It takes lots of time and practice before a dog will learn to replace a negative behavior such as jumping with a more appropriate behavior like sitting, and then offer it on her own. Practice in short, frequent sessions, whenever opportunities present themselves from day to day. Don't forget that you can prevent inappropriate activities from being an option—in the case of jumping, make sure you put your foot on the leash; this sort of prevention will enable your dog to be right more often.

### Quick Fix: Don't Generalize

Dogs are not good at generalizing their behavior. They don't automatically transfer it to other surroundings. Consequently, a dog might sit in the kitchen on the first try, but never sit at the pet store or in the park. If you want to have control over your dog's behavior anywhere, you have to train everywhere.

Once you pinpoint the causes and understand the triggers for your dog's inappropriate behavior, map out the changes you need to implement in your dog's routine, and then determine a time frame for training him. Set up a schedule of consistent practice times so that you teach each part of each behavior in small, digestible portions you can build upon every time you work with your dog. Be creative, make sure you provide for all of your dog's needs (mind and body), and find solutions that suit your dog's natural inclinations.

## Self-Control Exercises

Without self-control, your dog will never develop the concentration necessary for you to teach her basic obedience. Dogs don't learn self-control unless they are allowed to make choices and are rewarded for making good ones. Using a clicker and treats to mark and reward behavior is critical. The clicker allows you to mark the right choice and begin a bank account for the right behavior. The following exercise, Choose to Sit, is one example of helping your dog learn self-control.

1. Greet visitors with the dog on a leash.
2. If the dog jumps, the visitor goes away.
3. If the dog sits, the visitor stays and the handler clicks and treats.
4. The dog learns by trial and error how to get the person to pay attention to him.
5. The handler supplies information by clicking and treating the right responses.
6. The visitor supplies consequences for not sitting by not allowing the dog to say hello to her.

As you try to solve your dog's behavior problems, keep this example in mind. Learning will last longer when the dog figures out on his own what the rewardable behavior is, especially if the dog is usually excellent in the absence of distractions but falls apart in public.

The next example is a self-control exercise that helps your dog figure out how to pay attention to you. The Attention Game teaches your dog to check in with you often and to ignore distractions. In time, teaching your dog to check in with you will give him a greater awareness of you, which will improve his recall and heeling commands. (The Heel command teaches your dog to walk on your left side, regardless of your pace or direction, and to sit when you stop. You'll learn how to train this and other basic commands in Chapter 5.)

Dogs who have some responsibility to know where you are will not stray far away when they are off their leash. They will check in often and come back easily when you call because they know you are in control. Here's how the game works:

1. In a quiet room, sit in a chair with your dog on a leash.
2. Ignore your dog until she looks in your direction, then click and treat.
3. Ignore her again until she looks back at you, then click and treat.
4. Time yourself for one minute and count how many times she looks at you. If your dog looks at you six or more times in a minute, you are ready to add distractions.
5. Repeat this again in a new place or with a distraction and repeat the one-minute test. The distraction is too intense if your dog looks at you less than twice a minute.
6. Repeat this until your dog is looking at you six or more times a minute and then change the distraction again.
7. If your dog doesn't look at you more than twice in a minute for several repetitions, you will probably need to move away from the distraction or go somewhere less distracting.
8. Increase the quality and quantity of the rewards every once in a while to intensify the dog's response and to increase the likelihood that she will look at you more often.
9. Jackpot exceptional behavior. If your dog ignores an unexpected distraction, be sure to reward her with a whole handful of goodies to reinforce the good performance.

Your goal with this game is to focus your dog's attention on you. When your dog pays attention to you, he's learning to block out distractions and maintain self-control. Once he can do this successfully, you're ready to move on to more specific commands.

## Make a Plan and Chart Your Progress

As you shape your training plan, break down each behavior you teach into individual steps and track your dog's progress—and stumbling blocks. With each trick or behavior you teach, write each step down in sequential order and set small goals for each training session. Get in the habit of examining your dog's success rate and periodically re-evaluate your shaping plan, making adjustments as necessary.

Keeping your session short (less than ten minutes) with a clear goal in mind will help you determine whether you need to make things easier for your dog. Use the Ten in a Row rule as a general guide. Once your dog can repeat a step ten times with 100 percent accuracy, you are ready to progress to the next step. If your dog makes a lot of mistakes or acts disinterested, break things down into smaller steps or change your approach in some way.

Periodically review the behavioral questions explained earlier in this chapter with your family, and think about how you want your dog to respond in different situations. Remember to use your training log—it's an important part of a successful program, because your notes provide a bit of history on your progress. If you run into a snag along the way, you can review the steps where you were most successful, see what worked, and make changes so you can keep moving forward.

Lab Mix targets a
hand with his nose

Most importantly, stop reinforcing incorrect behavior and start reinforcing a better alternative behavior in its place. When choosing which behaviors to reinforce, remember the following things.

## Keep It Simple

Whatever you choose as the alternate behavior, it should be simple for the dog to offer quickly and reliably. Choose a single behavior, like Sit or Down, and reinforce it often. If the behavior is too complicated or involved, your dog might lose interest and revert to the undesirable behavior. A simple behavior like Sit is something you are likely to notice and reinforce even in a distracting environment. Be sure your dog knows the behavior well by applying the Ten in a Row rule.

## Plan Ahead for Success

If you want to ensure your dog responds to your commands everywhere, you have to train him everywhere. Learning in a variety of environments is more like real life for the dog, and the learning tends to become more permanent because the dog begins to realize that her commands work everywhere. Dogs pick things up quickly, but they're lousy generalizers. They tend to revert back to old, ingrained behaviors in new environments, so if you haven't taught your dog to sit when greeting strangers at the park, for example, he won't try that off the bat. The more distractions a dog gets to practice around, the quicker she will learn to generalize her response to your commands in all sorts of environments.

Always anticipate instances where you'll be able to reinforce the right behavior and prevent the wrong one. Keep a leash hanging by the door so that you are ready to thwart jumping on guests, and have a container of treats ready to reinforce sitting. Also carry your clicker and treats with you at all times. It might seem awkward at first, but it is essential for capturing and reinforcing your dog's behavior at the exact moment she makes the right choice. If you're ever not prepared to click and treat, then shower your pup with lots of praise and pats, or games and other opportunities to acknowledge her good behavior.

## Control the Variables

Distractions often ruin the best-laid training plans simply because they are too stimulating for a dog to ignore. Controlling the variables means controlling what's shifting your dog's attention away from you. Common variables include things that move, such as balls, off-leash dogs, cars, kids, and runners; environmental factors, like being outside; or the presence of food.

If you want your dog to succeed around distractions, it's essential to control the distance between your dog and the distraction, as well as manage the frequency, type, and intensity of the distraction. If you handle these things properly, you will increase the speed with which your dog learns. If ringing the doorbell sends your dog into a frenzy, for example, you might first want to work on desensitizing him to the doorbell sound; then you can move on to greeting the visitor. In this case, the dog's response to the doorbell and the dog's response to the person should be considered two separate issues.

You will immediately notice how important the distance between your dog and the action is during your training sessions, so find your dog's critical distance, and work from there. The distance at which he notices the distraction but will still perform the behavior is the starting point. Then, in subsequent training sessions, decrease that distance until he is able to work while the distractions are close to him.

Also pay close attention to the level of distraction you are working with. To decrease the intensity of a distraction, offer less movement, fewer dogs, people, kids, or other visual stimuli before attempting to teach the dog anything. As your dog learns to ignore distractions and perform the behavior well, you can gradually increase the intensity until he is working in the middle of the distraction.

Your goal over time is to train your dog to pay attention and respond regardless of what else is going on. Doing this in a slow sequence of progressions will help you attain your goals more quickly and reliably.

## Breed-Specific Behavior Problems

Dogs with persistent problems are often exhibiting behavior that is related to the job they were bred to do. When a dog has a behavior problem related to his original working ability, think of it as genetically hard-wired. Consider the Border Collie who chases and nips at heels, the Retriever obsessed with having everything in her mouth, or the Terrier who barks or chases squirrels. In these cases, genetic traits such as herding, retrieving, guarding, or chasing things that move come strongly into play.

Without the appropriate training and practice, it will be harder to stop a dog like this from practicing the undesirable behavior. If you are going to change your dog's mind about a behavior that is this instinctive, you need to provide extra reinforcement for the behavior you are trying to teach instead. Keep your standards low at first, and reward the dog for even attempting the new behavior. Don't up your criteria or expect multiple repetitions; simply reward the new behavior as often as possible. Each reward for the new behavior is money in the bank that builds reinforcement history to compete with a natural and self-rewarding behavior. Building a strong reinforcement history takes time and practice, but it can eventually replace old hard-wired behaviors with new desirable ones.

## Set for Success

It's human nature to notice what is going wrong and point it out. But pointing out mistakes only acts as reinforcement, and it can actually teach a person or animal to make the same mistake over and over again. An animal cannot change the past any more than you can; all you can do is make a difference in a future behavior by setting the animal up for success. Limit her options, prevent the wrong behaviors, provide good consequences for the correct choices, and follow through with consequences for the wrong ones. When an animal has choices, learning is more permanent and consequences will directly shape her response.

### Quick Fix: Tricks Work as Incompatible Behavior

The purpose of teaching a fearful or aggressive dog tricks is that when a dog is performing tricks—and is trained to ignore distractions—she is concentrating on something else. Think of this as another form of "incompatible behavior."

Behavior problems need not be a mystery. You *can* figure out why your dog behaves in certain ways and then devise solutions to teach your dog concentration, self-control, and obedience in order to redirect the behavior. By doing so, you won't become just another one of the many frustrated dog owners who give up and send their dogs to already overflowing animal shelters.

## Chapter 5

# Basic Commands

Basic obedience is essential to most tricks. The better your dog's response to commands like Sit/Stay and Down/Stay, the easier it will be to teach any trick, especially the more complicated ones. The basics of Sit, Down, Stay, Come, and Heel are foundation material for most tricks covered in this book. If nothing else, having some knowledge of the basics will help your dog to relax enough to learn something new. Teaching your dog how to sit or lie down can help you position her for success.

You can't just expect that working with your dog for a session or two will make her reliable around distractions and new people. If you want your dog to be well behaved and respond to your commands consistently, you must put in the time to train your dog. Spend time teaching these basics, at first in an environment with only a few distractions, and then build up to working somewhere outdoors or around other dogs or people.

## Sit

Teaching Sit involves luring the dog into position before you click and treat for the correct response. Remember that when using a lure, it's important to fade its presence quickly to keep the dog from becoming dependent upon it (see Chapter 3). Fading a lure is an important part of making sure your dog becomes reliable and is truly grasping the concept of sitting. The steps to teaching Sit are as follows:

**1.** Hold a treat slightly above your dog's nose and bring it back slowly over his head.

**2.** When your dog's bottom hits the ground, click and treat.

**3.** If your dog keeps backing up, practice against a wall so he can only go so far.

**4.** Repeat this until your dog is offering Sit readily.

**5.** Take the treat out of your hand and, holding your hand the same way, entice your dog to Sit. If he Sits, click and treat; if he doesn't, go back to using a food lure for six to eight more repetitions.

**6.** Once your dog is doing this reliably, verbally label the behavior "Sit" right before the dog's bottom hits the ground.

**7.** Repeat these steps in various places until your dog is responding well with no mistakes.

**8.** Now, without a treat in your hand, ask your dog to repeat the behavior more than once before you click and treat. Start with low numbers of repetitions like two, three, or four Sits before you click and treat, but don't follow a pattern.

**9.** To help him generalize the behavior, practice in new places— the pet store, the park, the vet's office. Remember that forgetting is a normal part of learning and you will need to go back to helping the dog, with a treat in your hand if necessary, if the place you are working is very distracting.

**10.** To test your dog's training, try for ten in a row. If he gets less than 100 percent, go back to practicing before asking for the behavior in that environment.

If your dog fails the Ten in a Row rule, you need to help him for a few repetitions before he attempts the exercise again without help. Going back to the previous steps to help your dog get into the right position gives him information about what he needs to do to earn his click and treat and prevents him from getting confused and frustrated.

### Trick Tips: Verbalize Effectively

When verbally labeling commands, it's important to use the right tonality, inflection, and volume. Never plead, mumble, or shout. It isn't necessary to use the dog's name first unless you need to get his attention because he's distracted. Remember that the tone you use to label the command while you are training is the tone your dog will respond to when you ask for the behavior in public. Experiment to find what tone and volume work best for you.

## Different Sits

If you really want to test your dog's ability to sit and stay, have your dog practice sitting on all sorts of strange-feeling surfaces—plastic bubble wrap, gravel, or a wire grate, to name a few. Place him in the sit if he refuses, then try a more normal surface such as wet blacktop, slippery linoleum, or sand. Next, ask him to "Sit" on something really comfortable, such as a thick rug, plush carpeting, or a pillow. Practice the sit on the most difficult surfaces first, then move to medium, and finally easy surfaces several times a day. Consider the command mastered when your dog willingly obeys the first Sit command all the time, even on the strangest surface.

## Sit/Stay

Turning the Sit into a Sit/Stay involves two processes: getting the dog to hold the position for longer periods of time (duration), and holding the position while the handler moves further away (distance). If you teach this behavior in two steps you will have a reliable dog who doesn't fall apart around distractions. The steps for teaching duration include the following.

**1.** Get your dog into a Sit and then count to two before you click and treat.
**2.** Gradually increase the time the dog has to hold the behavior by several seconds before you click and treat, until you can build it up to ten seconds between each click and treat.
**3.** When you can get to ten seconds, verbally label it "Stay" and give the hand signal (most people use a flat, open palm toward the dog).
**4.** Increase the time between each click and treat randomly to keep the dog guessing as to how long she must wait for her next click.
**5.** Add in distractions, and start from the first step to rebuild the behavior of Sit/Stay around new variables.

The second part of the Sit/Stay command involves the dog holding the Sit while you move away from her. The steps for teaching your dog to hold her position relative to yours are:

**1.** Get your dog into a sit and take a small step right or left, returning immediately. If your dog maintains her position, click and treat. If she doesn't, do a smaller movement.
**2.** Gradually shift your weight, leaving your hands in front of the dog. Click and treat the dog for maintaining her position in front of you. Practice this gradual movement until the dog is convinced she should stay in one spot.

Shetland Sheepdog sitting

3. Increase the distance slowly and keep moving at first, never staying in one spot too long without coming back to the dog to click and treat. Standing still too soon in the process will cause your dog to run to you.

4. As you are able to cross the room with your dog maintaining her position, start to stay away a few seconds longer before coming back.

5. Increase the time slowly so that you are combining both the length of time the dog holds the position (duration) and how close or far you are from the dog (distance).

## Down/Stay

When you are teaching your dog to Lie Down and Stay for extended periods of time, pay attention to the surface that you are asking him to lie on. Make sure it isn't extreme in temperature, and that it isn't so hard and uncomfortable that your dog fidgets and gets up a lot.

Short-coated dogs are often very uncomfortable on hardwood or linoleum floors, and will learn to lie down more readily on a carpet or towel.

**1.** Starting with your dog in the Sit position, use a treat to lure his nose about halfway to the floor. When your dog follows the treat by lowering his head, click and treat.

**2.** Gradually lower your hand closer to the floor. You might need to go back to a food lure for a few reps if your dog seems stuck and won't lower his head any further.

**3.** When you get the treat to the floor, experiment with holding it out under your hand, or closer to and under his chest, and wait. Most dogs will fool around for a while trying to get the treat and then plop to the ground. When your dog goes all the way down, click and treat.

**4.** Repeat this six times with a treat, clicking and treating each time your dog goes all the way down.

**5.** Now, without a treat in your hand, make the same hand motion and click and treat your dog for any attempt to lie down.

**6.** If your dog fails more than twice, go back to using a treat for six more times and then try again.

**7.** Take it on the road. When you go somewhere new or involve distractions like other dogs and people, the behavior might fall apart a bit. Don't be afraid to go back to using a food lure to show the dog what to do and then fade it out when the dog is performing the behavior reliably.

Some dogs have trouble lying down and seem to get stuck in the sitting position. Here are some tips for dogs who get stuck.

- Practice on a soft surface away from distractions at first.
- Use novel treats that the dog loves but hardly ever gets.
- Use a low table, the rung of a chair, or your outstretched leg to lure the dog low to the ground and under the object.

- Experiment with holding the treat closer to the dog's body and between the front paws close to the chest, or further away from her nose at a 45-degree angle.
- Avoid pushing on the dog to get her down. As soon as you start pushing and prodding, the dog turns her brain off and stops thinking about what she's doing, letting you do the work. If you want to teach your dog to think, don't push or pull her into position.

### Trick Tips: When Not to Use Your Dog's Name

Don't use your dog's name in conjunction with the Stay command. Since hearing his name implies he should be attentive and ready to go, in this instance, you would be sending a mixed message, which can confuse your dog. Whenever you use a verbal command, remember only to say it once!

## Come

Teaching your dog to Come when you call him has more to do with the status of your relationship than anything else you've done to this point. If your dog believes that you are in charge, he knows that you control everything good and that he must check in with you often in order to have access to the things he wants. Review the section on leadership earlier in this book and try to be diligent about becoming a strong and fair leader.

From a training perspective, the first thing a dog must do in order to Come is to turn away from what she wants and look back in your direction. To teach a strong foundation for Come, follow these steps:

1. Start with the dog on her leash in a slightly distracting area, keep her from the things she wants, and wait for her to look back at you, then click and treat.

**2.** Repeat this until the dog no longer looks away from you.

**3.** Change the distraction, go somewhere more stimulating, or go closer to the distractions and repeat.

**4.** If your dog doesn't look back at you in thirty seconds or less, move further away from the distraction until she will look at you within that time.

**5.** When your dog is looking back at you predictably, run backward as you click and deliver the treat at your feet to encourage the dog to catch you.

**6.** As your dog gets good at this, wait until she is on her way back to you before you click.

**7.** Verbally label this behavior "Come" as your dog gets to you to eat her treat.

**8.** Change the distractions. Increase the intensity of a distraction by going closer to it or increasing the distance between you and your dog by using a longer leash.

**9.** If your dog doesn't respond by looking back in a reasonable amount of time, don't be afraid to back away from the distraction.

The trick to teaching Come is to set your dog up to be successful. Don't allow off-leash freedom if your dog is not reliable, and practice, practice, practice! After establishing a firm foundation for Come on a six-foot leash, then use a longer leash, and go back and review all of the steps from the beginning. Some dogs will make great progress quickly, and others will need you to go much slower so that they can be successful.

Gradually increase the length of the leash until your dog can turn away from what he wants (the foundation for coming when called) and come back to you easily, then progress to dropping the leash and letting him drag it, and eventually take it off while reviewing all the steps to teach Come. When you first take off the leash, you might want to practice in a fenced or protected area in case you've hurried your dog's training and he runs off and won't respond. This just means that you need to back up a few steps and put the leash back on for a while.

### Quick Fix: Keep Your Hands to Yourself

When practicing the Come command, without realizing it, owners sometimes encourage their dogs to cut their approach and stay farther away by attempting to cradle, caress, or hug the dog. Some dogs are leery of anyone towering over them and associate your reaching with the end of their fun and time to go home. Teach your dog that your hug doesn't mean the end of your fun by putting the reward right between your feet, giving her a quick pat, and releasing her to go play again.

Though the process seems a bit long and tedious, it is well worth the effort, because you will have a dog who comes to you reliably when you call her. As your dog gets good at checking in with you, you can begin to offer real-life rewards mixed in with treats, like the freedom to go back to playing with another dog, the opportunity to sniff a spot on the ground, or the chance to chase a squirrel. If these opportunities are given as rewards your dog will learn that coming to you and checking in on a regular basis is a good thing. Regardless of how well your dog learns to come when called however, remember never to allow him off leash in unsafe areas where a mistake could cost him his life.

## Walking Without Pulling

Leash walking behavior is not something that's going to change overnight. Teaching your dog to Heel (walk at your side rather than drag you) requires lots of practice and repetition. Remember, pulling works, or has worked, for quite a long time for most dogs. A huge step in the right direction, therefore, is to stop following your dog when the leash is tight and she's pulling you. This might mean temporarily suspending all walks around the block so that she doesn't have the opportunity to practice pulling.

Managing your dog's behavior by not allowing her to practice it isn't teaching her to walk next to you, but it's a step in the right direction since she isn't being reinforced for the wrong behavior. Following are some tips for teaching loose-leash walking:

- Walk at a brisk pace and change direction frequently so that your dog has to pay attention to where you're going. The more you turn, the more your dog has to focus on you.
- Once you get the hang of walking and turning frequently, start to pay attention to the moment your dog turns to follow you, then click and treat him for catching up to you.
- At first, you might want to stop walking for a moment after the click so that the dog realizes what exactly he's getting clicked for. Use really delicious treats that your dog loves to keep his attention focused on you.
- Begin by practicing in a distraction-free place, and gradually go to busier places once your dog starts to understand what you want.
- Attaching a six-foot leash to your waist will keep your hands free for this exercise, so you will be able to click and treat your dog when he is next to you. The message you are sending to your dog is that pulling does not get him where he wants to go because when he pulls in one direction it makes you go the other way.
- For most dogs, the faster you walk the better, since a steady pace forces them to pay attention to where you are going next.
- Remember, the clicker is clearer and more precise than any other tool you can use to teach your dog what he's doing right. Using it to mark the behavior of being next to you will shorten your training time by half.

Since your dog has been pulling to get where she's going for as long as you've had her, the behavior is firmly established. To train her to choose to walk next to you instead, you will have to do lots of repetitions with particularly yummy rewards. Whether you use treats like roast beef, cheese, or chicken, or favorite games like tug or fetch, the important thing is that the dog wants the reward more than she wants to pull. Be creative and fun, and your dog will soon be trotting happily next to you.

### Quick Fix: On-Leash Games

Break up walking sessions with some fun ideas. For example, try playing the targeting game as you walk by having your dog touch your hand or pant leg with her nose, and don't walk a long distance all at once without changing direction or stopping frequently to make your dog Sit. These techniques are excellent ways for your dog to learn to control his enthusiasm while you are teaching him to walk properly on the leash.

### Adding Duration to Your Walks

Once your dog catches on to getting clicked for coming back to your side, raise the criteria by training him to stay there for a step or two before you reward him. Eventually, build the length of time the dog must walk next to you for several minutes, until he's no longer inclined to pull. Practice having him walk with you for different lengths of time around a variety of distractions, until he sticks close under any circumstance.

### Changing the Variables

Practicing proper leash walking skills in a new environment—with people, dogs, cars, bicycles, and other distractions—is critical to the reliability of this behavior. To help your dog to learn to stay with you despite distractions, change one variable at a time. There are two major variables involved in teaching your dog to heel: the distance to the distraction and the intensity of the distraction (this has to do with speed, noise level, and quantity). By controlling the variables and working slowly to introduce distractions while you maintain your dog's ability to heel, you will teach your dog to walk nicely on a leash regardless of the distractions around her.

Keep in mind that if you can't get your dog to perform the behavior, you are probably too close to the distractions and she can't concentrate. If this is the case, back away from the action until you reach a point where your dog will perform the behavior well. Then, once you're certain your dog can handle it, you can bring her closer to the action. Here are some reminders to help you set your dog up for success.

- Reduce the intensity of the distraction (quieter, slower, less of it) as needed.
- Use your best treats; training is difficult, so make it worth his while.
- Offer a high rate of reinforcement in a new environment.
- Slow the rate down (click and treat less frequently) when the dog starts to perform the behavior reliably, and for longer periods of time.

### Quick Fix: The Element of Surprise

Hide rewards all around your training area before your leash-walking session. It will be a huge surprise to your dog when she is unexpectedly rewarded with a delicious treat or an awesome toy that you pull out of the bushes. By hiding goodies everywhere, you'll hold your dog's attention and keep her guessing about what you're going to pull out next. This will make you more interesting to your dog, and it will make her more willing to learn to walk with you.

## Common Distractions

The type of distractions you are working around are also a huge consideration when you are teaching your dog to walk on leash properly. Following are the three major categories of distractions:

**1.** Things that move. These are the things that incite your dog's prey drive—her desire to chase after things that move, such as cars, bikes, squirrels, runners, dogs, motorcycles, balls, or kids. Every dog has a different level of distractibility, but most dogs find things that move irresistible.

**2.** Things that smell. The majority of dogs are motivated most of all by their stomachs, and for the hunting breeds especially, the "nose to the ground" behavior can be quite a challenge. Examples are food, animals, other animals' feces, and wildlife.

**3.** Things that make noise. Some dogs are more sensitive to sound than others. The average dog who is simply curious will get over it quickly and learn to ignore sounds if you change the variables, distance, and intensity slowly.

Whatever the distraction might be, it's always important to pay attention to your dog's excitement level and tone things down when necessary, so that he is able to absorb the lesson and learn properly.

## The Mule Impersonator

Often, slowpoke pups can be just as tough to teach as easily distracted, hyper dogs when it comes to leash walking. Laggards often plant their butts and will not budge with any amount of coaxing or cooing. There are several tricks you can use to get these dogs to follow you:

**1.** Put tension in the lead but don't pull. Make sure the leash is hooked to a regular collar, not a training collar.

**2.** As soon as your dog takes a step toward you to steady herself, be ready to click, treat, and lavish with praise.

**3.** Repeat this every time your dog stops. Don't go back to her; simply ignore the wrong behavior and pay attention to the right one instead.

**4.** Within ten minutes or so most dogs give up their stubborn-mule impression and go with you. However, some dogs might need several sessions before they give up, so remember to be patient.

### Trick Tips: Training Equipment

Keep in mind that training collars, head halters, leashes, and other devices are just that: devices. Their purpose is to manage pulling while you are teaching your dog to heel. The goal is for your dog to learn to heel with the help of training devices and then ultimately heel on her own whenever you ask her to, even when she's not on the leash.

## Get Ready to Do Some Tricks

Nothing beats the companionship of a well-trained dog. A dog who responds to basic commands is a dog who can be taken many places without putting you to shame—and a dog who is capable of learning more complex commands. Once your dog has mastered these basics, you're ready to gear her up for learning fun tricks.

**Chapter 6**

# Essential Trick-Training Tips

The more time you spend working with your dog, the more you are building up a history of "training equals fun!" Teaching your dog to perform tricks is a great way to help you get to know your dog and improve your relationship with him. Trick training is enjoyable, and most people love spending time training their dogs this way.

As you get started with a program of teaching your dog tricks, keep some essential points in mind: Training tricks, like any other type of training, takes time, patience, and practice. Be mindful of the considerations presented in the following sections, and you'll not only succeed in teaching your dog tricks, but also increase their quality. Also remember that trick training can be of great help when it comes to preventing other behavior issues your dog might have. By learning tricks, your dog will build a repertoire of positive alternative behaviors you can use to replace less desirable ones.

## Minimizing the Cue

In early trick training, the original cue you use to get your dog to perform is overexaggerated. When the trick is polished, change the cue to something subtler or change a verbal cue to a hand signal instead.

In order to change the original signal to a new one, the order in which you introduce the new command is very important. The standard practice for introducing a new label is: new cue followed by old cue. If you don't put the new cue first, the animal will ignore it and continue to respond to the old cue. You won't be able to get rid of the old signal unless the new signal precedes it.

Roll Over is a good example of a trick where you might want to abbreviate the original cue or replace it altogether. When you first start the training, you'd probably use a full arm circle type of motion close

Lab Mix holding his leash

to the dog's body to get him to throw himself over. You'd eventually want to shorten that to a slighter circular motion or even a closed fist.

## Working on the Quality of the Trick

Working on the quality of the tricks you teach is important. The qualities of distance, speed, and duration will help you polish your tricks and let you expand them to more elaborate performances. Distance pertains to how far away from your dog you can be and still have him perform the trick; speed refers to how fast he can execute it; and duration indicates how long he'll hold it.

The key is to work on improving one aspect of your dog's performance at a time. For instance, if you want to teach your dog to wave to you at a distance, you would not ask him to hold the wave (duration) for any longer than he normally offers it. Similarly, you would not work him at a distance if you were trying to work on the duration of the wave. Separating these variables of trick training will help your dog learn faster, more consistently, and more reliably.

### Distance

To increase the amount of space between you and your dog, you simply need to lower your standards for all other aspects of the trick except his ability to perform the behavior (however sloppy) at gradually increasing distances. Start with the dog close and reinforce him for gradually increasing distances. You will know if you have gone too far because he will make mistakes. This means you should shorten the distance to where he was reliable and continue more slowly.

Once you have him working reliably at one distance, go ahead and gradually increase it until you are satisfied with the performance. Don't be afraid to go back to the beginning if your dog falls apart and you lose the behavior entirely. If you go back to the beginning and start again, your dog will catch on more rapidly and give you an even better performance.

### Speed of Execution

The speed with which your dog performs a trick refers to the time between the moment you give the command and the time the dog actually starts to perform the behavior. To improve your dog's speed it is helpful to pick a number of seconds in which he has to perform the trick and only reward those repetitions that fall within your time limit. Anything more gets ignored. It takes most dogs only a short time to realize that it is how fast they perform the behavior that counts. Don't forget that if you are working on the speed with which your dog responds to the command, you should lower your standards for other aspects of the trick.

### Duration

This aspect also refers to time, but deals with the amount of time the dog must hold the behavior, such as leaving his paw up to wave, before you reward him. You can teach duration by delaying the click for varying amounts of time and only rewarding repetitions that are longer than average. As you increase the duration, go slowly so as not to lose the behavior altogether. If you increase the duration too fast and the dog no longer performs the behavior, go back to the beginning and start again. You will find that if you are flexible you will make an enormous amount of progress in a relatively short period of time.

## Teaching Tricks to Improve Behavior

Some dogs love learning tricks more than anything else, so they are more willing to work longer and perform with enthusiasm. If you enjoy teaching your dog tricks, use them in everyday life to help prevent your dog from practicing inappropriate behaviors. The following sections present some examples of ways you can use tricks to improve your dog's behavior. (You'll learn how to teach your dog all of these tricks in subsequent chapters.)

### Prevent Pulling

If your dog is a puller, try mixing in Roll Over, Sit Up, or Spin with reinforcing the dog for staying with you. In order to use tricks to replace problem behavior, not only does the dog have to know the trick very well in all different kinds of environments, she also has to be heavily reinforced (at least initially) for choosing to perform the trick rather than the inappropriate behavior. The more you practice what you want, the better it will happen for you when you truly need it. The more creative you are in your training program, the better your relationship with your dog will be.

### The Bark Stops Here!

Barking is a hot topic for almost every family with a dog. What is more maddening than listening to nonstop noise from your worked-up dog? Whether your dog is bored, unsocialized, fearful, or just too exuberant, there are several different tricks you can teach your dog to stop her barking. Teaching tricks such as Roll Over, Spin, Bow, and Wave will help to direct your dog's energy more appropriately

### Mugging Company at the Door

Jumping is a problem most dogs don't outgrow. Dogs mainly jump in their exuberance to greet a person and to welcome them to play. If you have a dog who likes to jump on people, teaching him an alternate greeting behavior can be an excellent solution. Teaching your dog to Roll Over and Spin one right after the other works well in this instance, as does requiring your dog to perform a Sit/Stay or Down/Stay before people are allowed to pet him. Or ask your dog to Play Dead or go Belly Up, and let the visitor scratch his belly as a reward. You can also have your dog go fetch a toy to keep his mouth busy and his feet off the company. Finally, a Go to Bed and Stay command can save his life by keeping him away from the open door and the big wide world beyond.

There is no quick solution to jumping, but preventing it from happening in the first place is a good place to start. Remember that dogs do what works. If something is no longer an option, it gets eliminated from the list of possibilities and is eventually replaced by what does work.

### Who's Walking Who?

Pulling on the leash is by far the number-one complaint from dog owners and the reason that they bring their dog to obedience class. Adding tricks to your dog's repertoire will help you manage her on-leash behavior and give you more options when she starts pulling. If she never knows what you might ask her to do next, she'll be more likely to pay attention to you and less likely to pull.

Teaching your dog appropriate leash manners can be time consuming and tedious, so break it up a little with some of these ideas:

- Play the targeting game as you walk by having your dog touch your hand or pant leg with her nose as you walk along.
- As you are walking, stop every so often and ask your dog to Spin.
- Don't walk a long distance all at once without changing direction, or frequently stopping to have your dog Sit.
- Mix up moving with Stop and Wave.
- Stop periodically and ask your dog to Roll Over several times in a row; it will take the edge off an excitable dog.

Using tricks while teaching your dog to remain under control on leash is an excellent way for her to learn to control her enthusiasm. Directing her energy toward more appropriate behavior will teach her to pay attention to you and what you are asking her to do. Remember that your dog has been pulling you along behind her for a long time. Since there is a lot of money in your dog's bank account for pulling, you'll need to counter that with huge jackpot deposits for *not* pulling. This requires frequent practice and a commitment to make sure you don't follow your dog when she is pulling you.

### Help for Fierce or Fearful Dogs

Aggression and fearfulness are two behavior problems that are stressful for both the dog and the handler. Keeping your dog from getting too overwhelmed and getting his attention back on you is your primary goal as the owner of a fearful or aggressive dog. Keep in mind that your ultimate goal is to give your dog a better association between the things he is afraid of and positive reinforcement. What better way to do that than to teach him to do tricks in situations where he normally reacts aggressively or fearfully? Try some of these options:

- Teach him to look at you for an extended period of time on command.
- Teach him to touch your hand with his nose.
- Teach him to touch an object or a person's hand (this has to be built up to slowly).
- Teach him to Spin or turn around.
- Teach him to Bow; this may help lighten up dogs that are passing by and help your dog feel more relaxed with their presence.
- Teach him to Wave.
- Teach him to Roll Over, which will disorient him enough that he won't know where the scary person or dog disappeared to by the time he's finished.
- Teach him to say Sorry, which will flatten him into a very submissive position—a great way to diffuse other dogs.

Applying these tools as you go about teaching your dog any trick you choose will make it fun and interesting for your dog to learn them. Concentrate on teaching the basics using these common methods before you start teaching tricks. Having lots of options will make it more fun for you to train your dog and more fun for him to learn what you want to teach him.

## Chapter 7

# Beginner Tricks

Now that your dog has made it through basic training, it's time to step up to simple tricks. Trick training will give both you and your dog a great sense of accomplishment. Teaching tricks does not need to be a complicated task. Even if you're a novice trainer, you can teach your dog an entertaining trick; this will boost your confidence as a trainer, and raise your dog's enthusiasm for working with you. The tricks in this chapter are simple and easy to teach. They're even appropriate for puppies who have a limited understanding of the training game.

## Tips for Teaching Simple Tricks

Each dog has a unique style of learning, and it is your job as her trainer to find the best techniques to explain whatever trick you are trying to teach to her. The amount of sessions needed to learn a particular trick will vary according to your dog. Just know that as long as you are progressing from one step to the next, you are succeeding. Here are some additional things to keep in mind as you work on new tricks with your dog:

- Introduce only one new skill per session. Skipping around too much will confuse your dog and might discourage sensitive dogs altogether.
- Remember that the shaping outlines are building blocks toward an end goal. As with most goals, teaching a trick is accomplished by starting at the beginning with the first step and progressing through to the end by adding each step, one at a time, until all the steps come together to form a trick.
- Once you've established a few basics, it's a good idea to review previous skills or steps as a warmup.
- Try to work in two or three sessions per day to see real improvement and accomplishment in a week's time. Make sure there's at least two hours between sessions. Dogs take time to process what they have learned and sometimes a rest gives them time to put more challenging concepts together.
- Be patient; even if you consider a trick simple, not all dogs pick up on every single trick quickly. Most dogs are willing to do anything if they understand what it is you expect from them, but they sometimes need more time to pick up on what you want.
- Don't label the behavior until your dog is performing it reliably with as little assistance as possible. A performance loses flash if it's bogged down with repeated commands and cookie lures.
- Don't forget to reward your dog with treats, toys, games, and affection. The more fun he has, the more willing he will be to work with you on tricks!

It is important to the overall flow of trick performance to be sure that your dog understands what is expected of him *before* you ask him to offer the behavior around distractions and on cue. Tricks that are simple and executed with a single cue are more impressive than more complicated ones performed with lots of added cues and lures from you. Remember, simple tricks can be made elegant when they are performed fluently.

You can teach the following tricks most easily using one of the three tools mentioned in earlier chapters—luring, free shaping, or targeting. It's also a good idea to review the basics often, to reinforce your dog's general skills before attempting to teach these tricks.

### Trick Tips: Polite Pawing

Many dogs can do the simple tricks that follow with very little prompting because they already use their paws to play with toys or get your attention. If your dog already likes to use his paws, teaching these tricks should be fairly straightforward.

## Give Your Paw

Give Your Paw may be the most natural trick for dogs prone to pawing. This one is especially important because it serves as the foundation for other paw-oriented tricks, so master it first. The shaping steps for teaching Give Your Paw are:

1. Find out what usually gets your dog to paw at you and use it to get him to do it. As your dog's paw is in the air, click and treat.
2. Repeat this fifteen to twenty times until your dog is offering his paw readily.
3. Now, leave your hand outstretched and wait your dog out; don't prompt him in any other way, just see what happens. If he lifts his paw at all, click and treat.
4. If after a few seconds he does not lift his paw, go back to helping him for another ten to fifteen repetitions before you try again.

You want your dog to understand that lifting his paw is what gets the click and treat to happen.

5. If you are using your outstretched hand as the prompt that gets your dog to give his paw, this can be turned into the cue for the behavior. Show your hand and click and treat your dog as he is stretching out his paw.

6. Add the verbal cue Give Your Paw when your dog is raising his paw to slap your hand on a regular basis.

7. Practice in different environments with various distractions, being careful not to overwhelm your dog. If the behavior falls apart in the new place don't be afraid to make things easier for him and help him out.

8. Avoid repeating yourself over and over; give one cue, wait for your dog's response, and click and treat. If your dog's response is not quick enough, go back to helping him for six to eight repetitions before trying again.

**Quick Fix: Encourage Your Dog to Give Her Paw**
If your dog does not usually raise her paw, try teasing her with a really yummy treat in your fist held at about nose height, scratching her on the chest, or touching her toenails with your finger. Most dogs will respond by raising a paw, giving you an opportunity to click and treat.

## High Five

The High Five is just a variation of the Give Your Paw trick with a few minor adjustments.

1. Teach your dog to target your hand with her paw for a click and treat (see Chapter 3).

2. Present your hand as the target in various positions until you can hold your hand up, palm facing the dog with fingers toward the ceiling. Click and treat your dog for touching your hand with her paw.

3. Practice this until your dog is quickly raising her paw when she sees you put your hand up.

4. Verbally label the behavior High Five when it is happening on a regular basis.

5. Add in distractions and work on having her do it with other people as well.

 Trick Tips: Mind Your Cues

Sometimes you'll want to use a different cue or hand signal than the one you started with when you are teaching tricks. There is an order that must be followed before your dog will perform the behavior on the new cue. You must present the new cue before the old cue or the dog will not pay attention to the new cue.

## Wave

Teaching your dog to Wave is not only adorable, it's also an effective way to boost doggie PR, because it gives him an appropriate way to greet people. Establishing an acceptable behavior, such as waving, is one of the keys to eliminating jumping on visitors. To perform this trick, your dog must raise a paw in the air while remaining stationary. You can teach him to do this by using a combination of targeting and shaping. The shaping steps are:

1. Start with your dog in a Sit/Stay and move a few steps away from him. Go back every few seconds for a full minute to reward your dog for not following you.

2. Standing in front of your dog, ask for his paw and click and treat him for giving it to you several times in a row.

3. Take a step away from your dog and ask for his paw. Click and treat the slightest effort to raise his paw without trying to move toward you. You may need to reward him for staying for a few repetitions before he'll remain in position and lift his paw.

**4.** As your dog raises his paw to place it in your outstretched hand, start fading this cue by removing your hand quickly. Click and treat your dog for swiping the air.

**5.** Repeat this step until your dog starts raising his paw when he sees your outstretched hand.

**6.** As your dog starts to offer swiping the air readily without moving forward, you can begin to verbally label this new behavior Wave.

**7.** Change the hand signal to an actual wave by changing the position of your hand from an outstretched palm to a waving hand. Offer the new cue (the waving hand) right before the old cue (the outstretched hand), gradually fading out the old cue until your dog is performing the behavior when you are waving at him.

**8.** Add in distractions and practice in new places until the behavior is reliable.

### Trick Tips: Calm Canines

Training involves many elements, but there are two things to remember. First, make the most of your dog's natural behavior by combining it with tricks that you put on cue, as the paw tricks demonstrate. Second, teach your dog the behavior you want him to perform, like sitting, in the presence of other people or dogs. The tricks in the following sections will help your dog remain calm, and will put your guests at ease, too.

## Bow

Teaching your dog to Bow on command not only makes for a flashy trick, it can also help you to put a visiting dog at ease. Dogs invite each other to play in this position and it can be an excellent way for your dog to learn to make friends. To perform this trick, the dog starts from a standing position and lowers the front half of his body until his elbows touch the floor.

1. Start your dog in a standing position; hold your hand below her chin (about 3 inches) and get her to touch your hand, then click and treat.

2. Gradually make it harder by placing your hand closer to the ground in increments of several inches each time. Click and treat your dog for making an attempt to lower her head further to touch your hand.

3. When your hand is resting on the ground, click and treat your dog for touching it with her nose without lying all the way down. If your dog continually lies down, raise your hand by several inches for a while before continuing.

4. Make sure you watch your dog carefully and click and treat any effort she makes to bend her elbows.

5. Once your dog will lower her top half, start giving her less help by removing your target hand before she touches it.

6. Fade the hand target until she drops her head when you just begin to make the motion with your hand.

7. Increase the difficulty by only clicking and treating those repetitions where she lowers her head fast.

8. Increase the difficulty by increasing the duration (length of time the dog holds the behavior) by adding a Hold It or Stay command. To increase the duration of the behavior, delay the click by one or two seconds and gradually increase the time.

9. Add a verbal cue like Bow just before she performs the behavior.

10. Take it on the road and perform in new places.

### Trick Tips: Click and Treat Frequently

In order to make progress in trick training, you need to work at a pace where the dog is getting clicked and treated frequently. As you increase the difficulty of a trick, try not to let the dog make more than two or three mistakes before you show him what you want him to do.

## Play Dead

Teaching your dog to Play Dead is a show-stopping trick that is sure to make even non-dog lovers sit up and take notice. This trick requires the dog to lay on his back with his paws in the air and hold it until released.

**1.** Get your dog to lie down, then click and treat.

**2.** Use a treat to roll your dog onto his side, then click and treat.

**3.** Fade the lure by doing six repetitions in a row and then trying the seventh repetition without the lure, clicking and treating the dog for performing the behavior.

**4.** Reintroduce the lure to get him to roll onto his back, then click and treat. Fade the lure after the sixth repetition.

**5.** Go back and put all three steps together so that he performs them all in one continuous motion for one click and treat.

**6.** Fade the lure by working with food for six repetitions then without food for two repetitions. Go back and forth until your dog responds the same with or without food. Note: The way you hold your hand will become the exaggerated cue that starts the behavior.

Shetland Sheepdog
playing dead

**7.** Change the old cue to a new cue by offering the new cue before the motion you used to get the behavior started. Pointing your thumb and forefinger like a gun and saying "bang!" is very flashy!

**8.** Work on speed by only rewarding the dog for quick responses to the new signal. Decide on how many seconds he has to start the behavior and click and treat even before he finishes. Clicking in the middle of the behavior is what builds speed.

**Trick Tips: Quick Review**
Stay with your dog first; then gradually give the cue for the behavior at greater and greater distances, only moving further away if the dog performs the behavior reliably. Don't be afraid to do remedial work with Stay if the behavior seems to fall apart.

## Belly Up

This is similar to the Play Dead trick except that it also involves allowing someone to touch the dog while she is flat on her back. Not all dogs are comfortable with this, so know your dog well before asking for it in front of strangers.

**1.** Have your dog Lie Down, then click and treat.
**2.** Lure your dog onto her side, then click and treat.
**3.** Lure your dog over onto one hip, then click and treat.
**4.** Lure your dog all the way onto her back, then click and jackpot (give a large number of small treats) the first time and quit the session.
**5.** Once your dog is rolling onto her back easily, fade the lure after six repetitions and see what happens. If the dog performs the Belly Up behavior, click and treat. If not, lure her six more times and try again.

**6.** When your dog is readily rolling on her back, call it Belly Up just before she offers the behavior.

**7.** Delay the click once your dog is in the Belly Up position by at first a few seconds and then more and more until she will hold the position for longer periods of time.

**8.** Add in touching her belly, and click and treat her for holding the Belly Up position while you do this.

**9.** Add in the distraction of strangers touching her belly, and click and treat her for holding the Belly Up position while being petted.

**10.** Take it on the road. Practice in new places with new people. Don't be afraid to help your dog into position if she gets confused in a new place.

### Trick Tips: Introduce an Audience

Although some of your training is behavior modification, some of it is just plain fun. Once you've trained a well-behaved, socially acceptable dog, let everyone in on the games!

## Roll Over

Roll Over requires your dog to lie down flat on his stomach, roll all the way over, and get back on his feet. Though the concept is simple, this is not always an easy trick for your dog to perform. Long-back breeds like dachshunds or basset hounds may not be as good at this trick as other breeds due to the way they are built.

### Trick Tips: Obstacles to Roll Over

Dogs with long backs sometimes find it uncomfortable and awkward to roll over on their backs and then try to get back on their feet. Overweight dogs or dogs that have had back injuries in the past may also have difficulties.

As you train this trick, pay close attention to your dog to be sure he's not hurting or twisting his back. If, despite your best efforts, your dog refuses to get on his back, skip this trick and try another. Your dog may be sore or uncomfortable and this may be his only way to express it. It is always important when training a dog to listen to what she is telling you!

### Trick Tips: Use a Soft Surface

If possible, teach the Roll Over trick on a soft surface like a towel or carpet so your dog is more comfortable.

1. Get your dog to lie down with his belly touching the ground, and click and treat.
2. Use a treat or a toy to turn your dog's head until he flops over on one hip, and click and treat.
3. Use a treat or toy held close to your dog's shoulder to get him completely on his side, and click and treat.
4. Gradually move the treat or toy, while he's chewing on it, to move him onto his back and then eventually all the way over. This step often takes many attempts before the dog is comfortable enough to be on his back.
5. Click and treat small efforts to move toward the treat at first before you get him to move further to get his click and treat. If you make it too hard to earn a click your dog will quit on you and think it's no fun.
6. When your dog is rolling over easily, it's time to start fading out all the extra cues and make him offer more before you click.
7. Once he can roll over with just this little bit of help you can begin to label this trick verbally as Roll Over. Whatever you are doing with your hand or fist could be a hand signal for the behavior as well.
8. Add in distractions one at a time and be prepared to help him complete the trick if he has trouble concentrating.

## Spin

Spinning involves your dog turning in a complete circle in either direction. As your dog gets good at this, you can have her keep spinning until you tell her to stop. You can teach spin with free shaping or a lure. For a beginner, it is probably easier to teach with a lure. You can see the results more quickly and will be more motivated to want to train more often. Feel free to add more steps to the shaping plan if you feel your dog needs more help in understanding what you want him to do.

 Trick Tips: Use a Target Stick

If you've tried to teach this trick using a lure or food treat, you probably realized how difficult it is to get rid of the lure. Instead, use targeting either with your hand or with a target stick to show your dog what you want her to do.

**1.** Use your hand as a target and with your dog facing you, get her to follow your hand a quarter of the way around, then click and treat.

**2.** Now, leave your target hand at the quarter-way mark and wait until your dog touches it with her nose on her own before you click and treat. Practice this until she's offering it readily.

**3.** Next, just before she touches your hand, move your target hand to the halfway point and click and treat your dog for following it, but before she actually touches it.

**4.** At this point, as you drop your hand she may spin the rest of the way around, but continue to click and treat for the halfway point in order to build speed.

**5.** Use your target hand to start the dog turning, but then pull it away quickly. Click and treat your dog for attempting to turn without the target to guide her.

**6.** Time the click so that you're clicking the dog for being at the halfway point.

**7.** Continue to minimize your target hand and click the dog for continuing to turn without your help.

**8.** Fade the target hand to just a motion to the left or right.

**9.** Fade the target to a simple left or right cue. A pointed index finger would be appropriate as a final signal.

**10.** Once your dog is beginning to spin as you start to move your hand, you can begin to add a verbal cue to your hand signal by saying "Spin" first, and then offering the signal.

Once you and your dog have mastered ten in a row, you can begin working on speed (see Chapter 6). Set a time limit in which your dog must perform the behavior, and click and treat only those repetitions that meet the goal. To train your dog to spin in the other direction, simply go back to the first step and work your way through.

### Quick Fix: Reworking Spin

If at any point the spin trick becomes slow or begins to fall apart, drop the verbal cue (don't ask for the behavior). Go back to luring your dog for a few repetitions, and then fade the lure until he is performing spin quickly and reliably. Add the cue back in when your dog's behavior is the way you want it.

## Are You Scared?

This trick will put a smile on everyone's faces, especially children's. To indicate his "fright," the dog runs under a table or bed and peeks out from under the tablecloth or bedspread. The shaping steps for teaching this trick are as follows:

**1.** Start with your dog under the table, and use your voice or a treat to get him to peek out. Click and treat.

**2.** Make sure you time your click for when he first pushes out from under the cloth.

**3.** Repeat this six to eight times and then try putting him under again and waiting to see if he offers peeking out on his own.

**4.** Once your dog has this part down, teach him to go under the table using a target lid (see Chapter 3 for teaching targeting with a lid).

**5.** Bait the target with a treat at first to encourage him to go under the tablecloth and click and treat each time.

**6.** Take the bait off the target but leave the target under the table or bed and send him again. Click and treat your dog for going under the table or bed after the target.

**7.** To get the peeking behavior, repeat the above step (getting him under the object) until your dog offers it readily and then delay the click. When your dog doesn't hear the click, he will probably come back out to see what's wrong. Click and treat him just as he peeks out from under the cloth.

**8.** Repeat this until he runs under and peeks out readily; then verbally label the behavior Are You Scared?

**Quick Fix: What if My Dog Doesn't Peek?**
If you're having trouble getting your dog to peek because he runs all the way out from under the tablecloth or bedspread, it means that you need to click sooner. An early click will catch the dog just as he is emerging and give him the idea that peeking is what is being clicked.

## Who's a Brave Dog?

This trick is similar to Are You Scared? except in this trick the dog runs around behind the handler and through his legs until she is looking up at the handler's face. The shaping steps to teach Who's a Brave Dog? are:

**1.** Starting with your dog sitting in front of you, use a target stick (see Chapter 3) to get your dog to go around you to the left or right.

**2.** Practice this until your dog will run behind your legs and touch the target for a click and treat.

**3.** Slowly move the target between your feet so that your dog comes between your legs enough to be able to look up at you.

**4.** Withhold the click after your dog starts to catch on to going through your legs and see if she will look up at you, then click and treat.

**5.** If your dog runs all the way through your legs, use the target stick to show her where to stop and click and treat her before she actually touches it.

**6.** You can label this behavior Who's a Brave Dog? by saying the label right before you give the cue that starts the behavior, like pointing or whatever you did to encourage the dog to go around you.

**7.** Slowly fade the target as your dog starts to offer the behavior readily by showing the target to get her started and then making the target disappear.

**8.** Add distractions and be sure to go back to helping your dog with the target stick if the behavior falls apart.

### Trick Tips: Social Graces

If your dog has learned to shake hands and bow, you're on a roll. Next, you can certainly expand his social skills to include a few kisses and pleasant conversation. The joy of having a dog is your interaction with each other. These next two behaviors really make the most of that.

## Kiss Me

Teaching this behavior utilizes a combination of free shaping and luring. You are catching the dog in the act of doing the behavior and rewarding it, but you are getting the behavior started by prompting it first. The shaping steps for teaching Kiss Me are:

1. Use food initially to excite your dog. This is key. Feed him a few small pieces of a treat and eat a few yourself, then stick your chin out and wait.

2. At the first sign of any attempt to open his mouth to lick you, click and treat.

3. Try putting the treats in your mouth and showing him they're there. Click and treat any attempt to lick you.

4. Add the verbal cue Kiss right before you think he's going to offer the behavior. Click and treat as the behavior happens.

5. Fade the food by showing it to the dog and putting it away on a counter or table and commanding Kiss. When he kisses, click and treat and run and get the treat.

6. Repeat this until the dog is beginning to offer the kiss as soon as you stick out your chin.

## Speak

Luring and free shaping, or a combination of the two, are the best tools for teaching this trick. The trick itself requires your dog to bark on cue.

1. Find something that causes your dog to bark, like a knock on the door or holding a treat out of range. Click and treat her when she barks.

2. Repeat at least twenty to twenty-five times.

3. Fake the antecedent to barking (the knock), and if your dog starts to bark, click and treat.

4. Verbally label the behavior Speak just before your dog barks.

5. Don't click and treat for any barking other than the one you ask for.

6. If she barks at inappropriate times, be obvious about turning your upper body away to let her know that extraneous barking will not be rewarded.

After basic obedience training skills (Sit, Stay, and Come), these simple tricks are the best opportunity for you and your dog to build a trusting and cooperative relationship. You'll develop a better understanding of how your dog thinks, and what motivates her, and your dog will learn to read your cues. Take the time to train your dog well; the benefits will last a lifetime!

## Ready to Learn More Tricks?

Regardless of your dog's skill level, anyone can have fun teaching these simple tricks. Remember, the bottom line is to make sure you have fun while spending time with your best friend. Whether you teach your dog tricks to entertain your friends and family or you do therapy work in hospitals and nursing homes, having a dog who can do tricks shows off all her amazing attributes. Spending time together learning something new will enhance your bond and strengthen your relationship, making the quality of life better for both of you. Hopefully, you will enjoy teaching these beginner tricks, and it will inspire you to move on to the more complicated tricks in the following chapters.

**Chapter 8**

# Retrieval and Delivery Tricks

Each of the tricks in this chapter involves your dog retrieving or picking up something in her mouth and then transferring it to another person. Any dog can learn to pick something up in his mouth and bring it to his handler. Although some dogs have an instinctive talent to perform this behavior, even the most reluctant dog can learn to retrieve using operant conditioning by means of a clicker and treats.

## Shaping the Retrieve

To shape the process of retrieving, break it down into tiny increments. Even dogs who are retrieving fanatics may refuse to pick up certain objects like keys or tools. Teaching a shaped retrieve using operant conditioning will not only make your dog a reliable retriever, it will also give you a strong base for teaching the retrieving tricks that follow in this chapter.

When shaping a dog to retrieve it is best to pick an easy object to start with—something the dog is likely to pick up on his own. If you're not sure what texture appeals to your dog, set out a bunch of objects and see which he chooses to play with on his own. Most dogs don't like to pick up metal and have difficulty picking up small objects that require them to smoosh their nose into the floor trying to get their mouth around it. Choose something your dog can get his mouth around easily, such as a face cloth, a retrieving dumbbell, or a small empty box.

### Trick Tips: Retrieving Dummies

When teaching your dog to retrieve, start with a novel object that is lightweight but is not a toy or ball. Retrieving dummies are ideal for this purpose. You can find them in pet supply catalogs.

Using a novel object will make it more likely that your dog will at least investigate it, giving you a starting point for shaping the retrieve. Teach the retrieve by breaking it down into the most basic steps. The more specific you are with the steps, the less chance the behavior will fall apart later. The shaping steps to teach the retrieve are as follows:

1. Put an item on the floor about three feet away from your dog.
2. Click and treat him for moving toward it.
3. Click and treat him for touching the object with his nose.
4. Repeat this step about a dozen times and then withhold the click.
5. If he mouths the object at all, click and treat.
6. Once your dog is mouthing the object, withhold the click until he picks up the object.
7. Delay the click once more and build the time he will hold the object.
8. Add distance by putting the object a short distance away at first and gradually increasing it.

**9.** Label the retrieve Take It as the dog is picking up the object.
**10.** Label the release of the object Give or Leave It.

Trick Tips: Retrieval Jackpot
Wait for your dog to get frustrated enough to close his mouth on the object before you click and treat. More than likely he will mouth the object quickly and release it, so be ready to click and give a jackpot.

## Links and Chains

As tricks get more complicated, you realize that one command really represents several behaviors—a behavior chain. In training your dog to perform these more complicated tasks, you can use two approaches: the behavior chain or back chaining. Really, the only difference is whether you start with first things first or work your way backward from a successful conclusion.

### Behavior Chains

The concept of a behavior chain is relatively simple: A behavior chain is simply the breakdown of what the dog has to do in order to complete the behavior. For example, in order for your dog to bring his leash to you on the command Go Get Your Leash, he must: know where to find the leash; take it in his mouth (which may mean picking it up off the floor or pulling it from a doorknob); carry it to you in his mouth; and release it into your hand. Each of these steps is a link in the behavior chain, which is only as strong as its weakest element.

Trick Tips: Comfortable Retrieving
Make sure your dog is comfortable retrieving all of the objects you give him. If the retrieving part of the trick is weak because the dog is not comfortable retrieving a particular object, the performance of the trick will become sloppy and unreliable.

If your dog doesn't know how to carry objects without a lot of extra commands and prompting, behavior-chain tricks will be choppy and uninteresting. Breaking things down into their component parts is a way of simplifying the trick and improving your dog's performance.

## Back Chaining

Back chaining is related to behavior chains except instead of training step 1, step 2, step 3, and so on, you train it backwards, step 3, step 2, step 1. The idea is that if you train something backwards your dog will perform the behavior more reliably and with greater speed and enthusiasm because he is moving toward something he already knows well. By teaching him a multi-step task backward, you are helping him to remember the steps more easily because he learned the last one first. So in the case of the trick Bring Me Your Leash, the sequence would be: Hold the leash and release it into my hand; carry the leash to me from a distance; take it in your mouth; go find it.

Each of these steps may need to be broken down further to meet your dog's individual needs, but the basic concept is the same. When the dog performs the whole trick, he will be moving from less familiar steps to more familiar steps. Because he learned the last part of the trick first, he will be more confident and flashy as he gets to the end and more reliable overall in his performance of the trick.

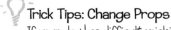 Trick Tips: Change Props

If your dog has difficulty picking up any of the props you are using, don't be afraid to go back to the basic steps of the retrieve using the new object. You will find that going back to kindergarten will help your dog's overall grasp of retrieving and will make her less likely to refuse to cooperate.

## Go Get Your Leash

This trick involves having your dog retrieve his leash and bring it to you. To make this easier on your dog you may want to have one place where you always leave your dog's leash, such as on a doorknob or by the front door. Your dog has to go to where the leash is kept and pull the leash off with his mouth. He then needs to carry the leash to you and hold it until you take it from him.

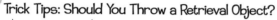

**Trick Tips: Should You Throw a Retrieval Object?**
The object of the exercises in this section is to train your dog to retrieve specific, stationary objects. Throwing objects, as you would in fetch, puts your dog into prey drive, a highly charged emotional state. It is best to leave the object stationary and let him figure out by your clicking which behaviors are rewardable and which are not.

If you teach this trick and the following behaviors using back chaining, you will find it easier for your dog to perform them because he is always moving toward the more familiar steps.

1. Hold the leash out and ask your dog to take it. Click and treat the exact moment he puts it in his mouth.
2. Back up a step and see if he will follow you; click and treat him for moving with the leash in his mouth.
3. Put the leash on the floor and tell him to Take It. As soon as he picks it up, click and treat.
4. Put the leash on the floor but don't click and treat until he takes it and takes several steps toward you.
5. Put the leash in various places at various distances and repeat. Click and treat your dog for taking it under these new circumstances.
6. Gradually move the leash to where your dog can expect to find it and click and treat him for going to that spot.

**7.** Replace the Take It cue with Leash, by saying the new cue Leash right before the old cue. Gradually fade Take It so that your dog will perform the behavior on the new cue.

**Trick Tips: Special Items**
When you are training for retrieving exercises, use an object that you can put away when the session is over. Keep the item "special," so that your dog looks forward to working with it every time you practice.

## Get the Mail/Newspaper

This trick works well if you have a door slot for your mail or you have a daily newspaper that gets delivered to your door. For this trick, your dog has to go to where the mail or paper is kept, pick up the item, bring it to you, and release it into your hand.

**1.** Teach your dog to carry nonessential letters and junk mail without stopping to shred them before you use the real thing. ("The dog ate the mortgage bill" probably won't go over well with your spouse.) Do this by clicking and treating your dog for taking the letter or newspaper and holding it without mouthing it.

**2.** Take a step or two away and have her bring it to you. Click and treat the motion of moving toward you.

**3.** Put the letter on the floor and tell your dog to Take It. You may want to use junk mail for this part until your dog refines her techniques in picking up something so close to the floor.

**4.** When your dog is retrieving well, begin to work her with the real mail pile or newspaper.

**5.** Label this behavior Mail or Paper by saying this new cue right before the current cue Take It; pretty soon your dog will be fetching with enthusiasm and finesse.

## Go Find the Remote

Visitors—especially those who have only a mild interest in dogs—love this trick. Guests are impressed when a dog can serve a useful purpose. If your housemate tends to hog the remote control, your dog can be your advocate in getting it back with a smile. For this trick, the dog has to find the remote, pick it up, carry it to you, and drop it in your hand.

**1.** Hand your dog the remote and click and treat him for holding it.
**2.** Back away a step or two and click and treat him for carrying it to you.
**3.** Put the remote on the couch or coffee table and tell your dog to Take It. Click and treat him for picking it up in his mouth.
**4.** Send him into the living room at greater distances and click and treat him when he finds the remote.
**5.** Call him to you as he gets the hang of this and click and treat him for holding it until you reach out to take it.
**6.** Replace Take It with the command Remote by offering the new cue right before the old cue.

## Go Get the Phone

Nothing is better than having your own personal answering service. For this trick your dog has to retrieve the phone and bring it back to you. You may want to use a cordless phone for this (unless you sit close by) and store it on a low table or the floor to make it easy for your dog to reach it.

**1.** Hand your dog the receiver and tell her to Take It. Click and treat your dog for taking it in her mouth and holding it for a few seconds.

**2.** Hand your dog the phone and back away from her, encouraging her to follow you. Click and treat her for carrying the phone to you. Make sure the click happens while she is moving toward you, not when she arrives.

**3.** Repeat this step again, but now click and treat your dog for delivering the phone to you.

**4.** Put the phone on the floor and ask her to Take It; click and treat her for picking up the phone.

**5.** Put the phone at greater distances and have her retrieve it from farther away. Time the click and treat for when your dog puts her mouth on the phone.

**6.** Increase the difficulty by delaying the click until she has the phone and is turning back to you. You can use a voice prompt like her name or the Come command.

**7.** Label the behavior Go Get the Phone by saying it right before the commands Take It and Come, until you can gradually fade the old commands and replace them with the new command Go Get the Phone.

**8.** Practice in short sessions until your dog begins to move toward the phone on the command Go Get the Phone.

### Quick Fix: Use an Old Phone First

Using a cordless phone for this trick is ideal. However, if you're afraid your dog might chew your good phone to shreds, you might want to start practicing with the receiver from an old phone first. Switch to the real phone once your dog is reasonably good at picking up the receiver without damaging it. Also make sure the real phone is easily accessible to prevent your dog from dropping it or knocking it off the table.

Golden Retriever holding
his dinner bowl

## Go Get Your Dish

This trick is a great way to show off your dog's intelligence. You'll probably want to keep his food dish in one spot so that he knows where to go to get it. For this trick your dog goes and brings his empty dish to you. Some dogs find it hard to retrieve metal dishes, in which case you may want to use a plastic one instead. The shaping steps are as follows:

1. Hand your dog his dish and tell him to Take It. Click and treat him for holding the dish.
2. Take a step away and call him to you. Click and treat him for moving toward you with the dish in his mouth.
3. Put the dish on the floor and tell him to Take It; click and treat him for picking up the dish.

4. Now, repeat this step but back away and click and treat the dog for picking up the dish and moving toward you.

5. Put the dish closer and closer to where you normally keep it, and send him to take it over greater distances.

6. As your dog gets good at this replace Take It with the new verbal cue Want to Eat? by saying the new cue right before the old cue, until the dog starts the behavior on the new cue.

### Quick Fix: Re-teach the Retrieve for Metal Objects

Some dogs hate having anything metal in their mouths. If you do want your dog to use a metal dish, don't be afraid to go back to kindergarten and re-teach a retrieve with the metal object. See the shaping steps for teaching the retrieve and substitute the object with the metal bowl.

## Find My Car Keys Please

If you are a person who constantly loses her keys, this trick may save you a lot of time. For this trick your dog has to locate your keys by using her eyes and sense of smell, pick them up, bring them to you, and release them to your outstretched hand. The shaping steps are as follows:

1. Hand your dog your keys and tell her to Take It. Click and treat her for holding your keys.

2. Take a few steps back and call her to you. Click and treat her for moving toward you with the keys in her mouth.

3. Put the keys on the floor and tell her to Take It; click and treat her for picking up the keys.

4. Repeat the previous step but back away, and click and treat her for picking up the keys and moving toward you.

5. Put the keys in different places at varying distances and click and treat your dog for finding them. Vary where you put them,

sometimes leaving them out in the open, sometimes leaving them concealed.

**6.** Gradually work it so that your dog is actively searching for your keys. When you are at this point, go ahead and label it Keys. Replace Take It by giving the new cue Keys right before the old cue. Then, gradually fade the old cue.

**7.** Practice this one frequently to keep your dog motivated about searching for your keys.

## Put Away Your Toys

This trick will impress your more practical friends who don't have dogs. A dog who picks up his own toys beats the heck out of a spouse or child who can't find the laundry hamper or put his dirty dishes in the sink. For this trick the dog has to pick up one toy at a time and put it in his toy box or basket. The shaping steps are as follows:

**1.** Hand your dog a toy and tell him to Take It; when he has the toy in his mouth, click and treat him for holding it.

**2.** Put the toy box between your feet and encourage the dog to come to you; click and treat him for holding the toy over the top of the box.

**3.** Repeat the above step, but ask the dog to Leave It as he holds the toy over the box.

**4.** Put the toy on the floor and tell him to Take It; click and treat him for picking up the toy.

**5.** Repeat the above step with more than one toy on the floor at a time.

**6.** Replace the Take It and Leave It cues with the new cue Toys Away by saying the new cue right before the old cue. Gradually fade the old cue.

## Trick Tips: The Secondary Skill of Delivery

The fundamental skill involved in retrieval tricks is the dog's ability to pick things up in his mouth. The secondary skill is the dog's ability to carry things in his mouth from one place to another. Delivery tricks simply change the "from" and "to," which, as these next few tricks will show, can be fun **and** functional.

## Bring This to Daddy

This trick is great for dogs looking for a job to do. Having your very own canine delivery service is an excellent way for your dog to earn his keep. For this trick your dog has to pick up an object—a note, a tool, or any item reasonable for her to carry—and take it to someone else in the house. The shaping steps are as follows:

1. Hand your dog an object, using the command Take It, and have the helper call her from a step or two away. Click and treat her for moving toward that person.

2. Gradually move the helper greater and greater distances and click and treat the dog for moving away from you and toward your helper.

3. Gradually fade out the helper calling the dog, having the person go out of sight.

4. Replace the Take It command with Bring This to Daddy (or whatever your helper's name is) by saying the new cue right before you say Take It. Click and treat the dog for taking the object and moving in the direction of the helper. Gradually fade out the old cue.

5. Vary the objects you have the dog carry, and practice often. This is the type of trick that gets better the more you practice it.

## Mail a Letter

Teaching your dog to mail a letter is a fun and functional trick that uses lots of energy and is very entertaining to watch. Your dog must take a letter in his mouth, jump on the mailbox, and push the letter through the slot. He will need you to pull down the lever for him so he can drop the mail in the right spot. This trick is probably best taught to dogs tall enough to reach the top of the mailbox, unless you give your little one a boost. The shaping steps for teaching this trick are as follows:

1. Using the Touch command, ask your dog to use his nose to push the letter into the slot. Click and treat him for touching his nose to the letter.
2. Withhold the click and treat until he pushes the letter a little further in the slot this time.
3. Have him put two front paws on the mailbox and click and treat him for staying up for gradually longer periods of time. If you have a small dog, you may want to hold him close to the box and click him for putting his feet on the top.
4. Hand your dog a letter and tell him to Take It. Click and treat him for taking the letter, then for holding the letter for longer periods of time.
5. Call him to put his paws on the box while holding the letter, and click and treat.
6. Work on this step until the dog is easily balancing on his hind legs while holding the letter.
7. Now try to get the dog to leave the letter on the tray by telling him to Leave It and clicking and treating him for letting the letter go. You may need to adapt this trick for small dogs by holding them close to the box.

8. Practice all the steps until the entire trick is fluid and the dog responds to your command Take It by following through with all the other steps.

9. Replace the cue Take It with the new cue Mail It by saying the new cue right before the old cue and gradually fading the old cue.

## Throw This in the Trash

Teach your dog to pick up anything you point to, including soda cans or other household items. This retrieving trick requires your dog to pick up the trash and release the object into a trash bin. To make it easier for your dog to get the trash into the container, you will probably want to use an open or swing-top trash bucket that is no taller than your dog's elbows.

**Trick Tips: Don't Overturn the Trash Basket!**
Consider the height of the trash basket and its opening when you are teaching this trick. The height of the basket needs to be proportionate to the dog's head so the opening is easily accessible. As you add distance to this trick you may want to even weight the basket so that it doesn't tip and scare the dog.

1. Work with your dog and have her retrieve many different kinds of trash items; have her bring them to you over increasingly longer distances.

2. Sit on a chair with the trash bucket between your feet. Tell your dog to pick up an item using the Take It cue, and call her to you; click and treat her when she is as close to the opening of the bucket as she'll come.

3. Repeat this step but delay the click by a few seconds until she is eventually standing with her chin right over the edge of the bucket.

4. With your dog standing close to the bucket, tell her to Leave It and click and treat her for releasing the trash. You will need to practice this so that your dog will eventually release the item right into the trash bucket.

5. Experiment by withholding the click until your dog makes a deliberate effort to drop the item in the bucket.

6. Label the behavior Throw It Away by saying this new cue right before the old cues Take It and Leave It. You will have to practice this many times before the new cue initiates the behavior.

7. Practice with different items so that your dog will retrieve and discard just about anything you ask her to.

### Trick Tips: Take It to the Next Level

Just when you think you've covered all sorts of tricks—there are still more games and tricks to keep you and your pet learning new things together. These games are great to play in all sorts of places—in the backyard, at the beach, or in the living room. Your dog is part of your family; if he's well trained and well behaved, he will get invited more places and will be more fun to be around.

## Let's Play Ring Toss

This old-fashioned game is a wonderful way to occupy a high-energy dog. You can buy an inexpensive ring-toss game in any toy or department store. For this trick the dog has to pick up each ring and place it on a post one at a time. This behavior is repeated until all three rings are on the post. The shaping steps for this trick are as follows:

1. Hand your dog a ring and click and treat him for holding it.

2. Put the pole close to you and have your dog deliver the ring close to the post; click and treat him for releasing it over the post.

**3.** You may help the dog by tapping the post and encouraging him to drop it. Click and treat him for gradually closer attempts to leave the ring close to the post.

**4.** Withhold the click and treat and only click attempts to put the ring on the post.

With patience and time this can be a very entertaining game for your dog to play.

## Sea Hunt

For this trick your dog has to fetch things out of a body of water. You can use a baby pool, the bathtub, a bucket, or a lake or pond. The dog's goal is to retrieve all the items you sink or float and bring them back to dry land. This is a terrific warm-weather game because it gives your dog a fun way to cool off. Fill up a baby pool with a few inches of water, depending on your dog's size, and sink some treasures for her to retrieve. The shaping steps for teaching your dog to play Sea Hunt are as follows:

**1.** Hold the object on the surface and ask the dog to Take It. Click and treat her for putting her mouth around it.

**2.** Hold the item just below the surface and click and treat the dog for dipping her nose under and taking it.

**3.** Gradually hold the item deeper until the dog is snagging it off the bottom.

**4.** Vary the types of things you have the dog retrieve and keep the game light and fun.

**5.** Vary the depth of the water as your dog gets better at this game to make it more interesting and fun for everyone involved.

## Achoo! Can I Have a Tissue?

This one is really a crowd pleaser. To perform this trick your dog has to retrieve a tissue on a sneeze cue. And who wouldn't be amazed by a dog who gets you a tissue when you sneeze? For this trick you need a popup box of tissues and a convincing fake sneeze. The shaping steps for teaching this trick are as follows:

1. Hand the dog a tissue and click and treat him for taking it and holding it.

2. Take a step away and have him bring it to you. Click and treat him for moving toward you with the tissue in his mouth

3. Introduce the tissue box by pulling a tissue out and laying it across the top of the box. Click and treat him for taking the tissue off the top of the box.

4. Gradually tuck the tissue in so that the dog has to pull the tissue out to get his click and treat.

5. Replace the old cue Take It with the new cue Achoo! by saying the new cue right before the old cue. Click and treat the dog for starting the behavior as you sneeze.

### Quick Fix: What if Your Dog Is a Shredder?

You can teach your dog to grab a tissue without tearing it in a million pieces by giving her lots of opportunities to practice, and by not letting her hold the tissue for too long. It might also be a good idea to keep the tissue box in one place so the dog knows where to go to get a tissue when you sneeze.

Retrieving tricks are some of the most impressive because they involve several steps and highlight a dog's ability to think things through and put together a great performance. While each trick involves different props, they all involve the same basic skill of being able to pick something up and carry it back to you. Reviewing the basic retrieve with the new item is a great way to warm up any new trick regardless of how experienced your dog is.

### Trick Tips: Get the Retrieving Show on the Road

Take retrieving on the road right away. Performing retrieving tricks in public is difficult; if you practice in different places from the start, your dog will be comfortable retrieving anywhere.

## Chapter 9

# Super-Smart Tricks

We all have a bit of a showoff in us, and dogs are no exception. Dogs love to make us laugh, and their antics often cheer us. And some dogs, because of their breeds or their personalities, seem to be particularly suited to elegant tricks. That's why it's important to know your dog and understand her—so you can train her to her best advantage. Taking the time to work with your dog will strengthen your bond with her and fine-tune your ability to communicate with each other.

This chapter will show you how to teach a number of fancy tricks, for dogs who are really ready to ham it up. Your dog will love strutting her stuff!

## Show Me Your Best Side

When your dog is performing this trick, she looks as though she is posing for a picture. This trick requires your dog to turn her head to the side and hold it. The easiest way to teach this trick is by free shaping, which means limiting your dog's options and catching the right behaviors with a click and treat to shape the dog into the actual position that you are looking for.

1. Start with your dog facing you in a Sit and click and treat her for staying.
2. After about thirty seconds or so, stop clicking and watch her closely; if she turns her head at all, click and treat.
3. Pick one side or the other to start with and click any head turns in that direction.
4. When your dog starts to understand that turning her head is causing the click, it's time to delay the click by a few seconds to encourage her to hold the position.
5. Gradually increase the seconds by a few at a time until your dog will turn her head to the side and hold it for fifteen seconds.
6. Label the behavior Pose just before she offers the turn of her head. Repeat until the command Pose causes the behavior.

## Push a Baby Carriage

This trick is adorable, but for safety's sake it should not be practiced with a real baby. A doll carriage with a baby doll is safer. This trick requires the dog to stand and walk on his hind legs while pushing the carriage with his front feet. The shaping steps for teaching Push a Baby Carriage are as follows.

1. Get your dog to sniff the baby carriage, and click and treat.
2. Secure the carriage so that it won't roll, and use a target to get your dog to put his front paws on the handle; click and treat.
3. Get your dog to hold the position by delaying the click and treat by a second or two.
4. Fix the carriage so that it will roll only a short distance (use blocks of wood behind the wheels), and click and treat your dog for moving the carriage a little at a time.

5. Encourage your dog to move the carriage and click and treat him for complying.

6. Control how far the carriage rolls to avoid scaring your dog.

7. You can label this behavior Push by saying this cue as the dog is moving the carriage.

### Quick Fix: Don't Tip the Carriage!

To prevent the carriage from tipping, weight the seat with some heavy books so that when your dog jumps up to touch the handle the carriage stays stable and stationary. Be sure the wheels are locked or use wood blocks to prevent the carriage from rolling away too soon.

## Hi-Ho Silver, Away!

This trick, inspired by a horse-loving friend of mine, is a great way to show off a dog who likes to jump up on you. The only difference is your dog is not making physical contact with you when she is holding the rearing-horse position with her front legs stretched upward. The shaping steps for teaching Hi-Ho Silver, Away! are as follows:

1. Hold your hand as a target above your dog's head and click and treat her for touching it.

2. Gradually raise your hand until she is all the way up on her hind legs.

3. Practice frequently to help her build up her leg muscles.

4. Get your dog to hold the position by delaying the click and treat for several seconds.

5. Increase the time by a few seconds until she can hold the position for about fifteen seconds.

6. Cue your dog to extend her paws by using the Paw It command with your hand as a target.

7. Only click and treat versions of this behavior that are of longer duration and the right position (front paws extended).

8. Fade the hand target by using it to start the behavior and then pulling it away. Click and treat your dog for continuing to perform the behavior in the absence of the target.

9. Replace the old cue with the new cue Away by saying the new cue right before the dog starts the behavior.

## Sit Up Pretty

For this trick the dog sits on his hind legs with his front paws tucked into his chest. This is also a behavior that the dog needs to practice frequently to be able to build up his back and hind-end muscles. The shaping steps for teaching Sit Up Pretty are as follows:

1. Use your hand as a target and click and treat him for touching your hand while raising his front end off the ground.

2. Withhold the click and treat by a few seconds to get your dog to hold the position high enough to have him sitting up on his back end, but not standing.

3. Add a cue like Sit Up or Beg, by saying it right before the Touch cue.

4. The click and treat should happen as soon as the dog starts the behavior on the new cue.

### Trick Tips: Hand Fade

Practice fading your hand as a target by presenting it but clicking before your dog actually touches it. By clicking your dog early so that she is on her way to touching your hand but doesn't actually make contact with it, she will be less dependent on its presence and it will be easier to fade.

## Balance a Cookie on Your Nose

This trick demonstrates your dog's will power, because she must balance a cookie on her nose and wait to take the cookie until you say so.

1. Start with your dog in a Sit in front of you and click and treat her for staying.

2. Practice holding her muzzle and placing a cookie on her nose for a click and treat.

3. Repeat this last step until the dog can hold still for several seconds.

4. Slowly let go of your dog's muzzle and click and treat her for holding it steady.

5. Gradually increase the amount of time your dog balances the cookie on her nose before you click and treat.

6. You will probably find after a bit of practice that your dog develops a flip-and-catch technique to eat the cookie. This makes the trick all the more flashy and impressive.

### Trick Tips: Humble Dogs

Although some dogs are prone to fancier tricks, others are, by nature, more sedate. These simple and adorable tricks suit more sedate personalities, and will therefore be easier for you to teach. How you use the tricks, such as Say You're Sorry, is entirely up to you.

## Say You're Sorry

For this trick your dog lies down with his chin on the ground between his front paws. For an added bonus, teach him to look up at you, which will add an even more convincing element to the performance. You may want to use this as the canine version of Time Out.

1. Put your dog in a Down, facing you; click and treat him for holding that position.

2. After about thirty seconds, withhold the click and wait. Pay close attention and click and treat any head motion down.

3. Once your dog starts to understand that lowering his head is what causes the click, withhold the click until your dog holds the position for an extra second.

German Shepard
saying he's sorry

4. Increase the number of seconds your dog has to keep his head down until you can build it up to fifteen to twenty seconds.

5. Label the behavior Sorry by saying the command right before he offers the behavior.

6. Repeat this step until the command Sorry triggers the behavior.

**Quick Fix: Get Your Dog to Look Down**
To help your dog understand that lowering his head is what is causing the click, deliver the treat low to encourage the dog to look down. This will give you more opportunities to reward him for offering the right behavior.

## Say Your Prayers

Whether they are praying for leniency after getting into the garbage or praying for mud to roll in, any dog looks cute performing this trick. This trick requires your dog to rest her paws on a chair or stool and tuck her head between her front paws. She can be sitting or standing when she does this.

1. Use a table, stool, or chair that won't move when your dog puts her paws on it.

2. Get your dog to put her front paws on the stool by tapping the stool or luring her with a treat. Click any effort to get her paws up on the stool.

3. Delay the click so that your dog is putting her paws up and leaving them there for three seconds before you click and treat.

4. Using a yogurt lid as a target, get your dog to put her head between her front paws by placing the target slightly under her chest. Click and treat your dog for making attempts to touch the target.

5. Delay the click again until your dog holds her nose to the target for longer periods of time.

6. Fade the target slowly by clicking before she actually touches it, or by making it smaller.

7. Label the behavior Say Your Prayers as she is performing the behavior, just before any other cues. Gradually fade any old cues.

### Trick Tips: Prevent Sliding

To make the trick Say Your Prayers go more smoothly and to prevent your dog from scaring himself, choose a low stool that he can put his paws up on easily—one that won't slide across the floor when he leans on it. Also consider doing this trick on a rug or putting nonskid material under the legs of the stool.

## Ring a Bell

This trick involves teaching your dog to ring a bell with her nose or a paw. This trick is also quite practical, as you can teach your dog to ring a bell when she wants to go outside to the bathroom.

### Trick Tips: Patience Goes a Long Way

You learned earlier that dogs can be trained to perform any task that they are physically capable of doing. That said, the critical factor to performing the following tricks successfully is your patience in handling your dog. Using the skills you learned in Chapter 3 and your knowledge of chain methods from Chapter 8, start training your dog for these actions when you see that she is ready.

Hang a set of bells next to the door that you normally use to let your dog outside. Once she learns how to ring the bell with her mouth or nose, start having her do this each time she goes out to go potty. Pretty soon your dog will ring the bell to let you know she wants to go out.

**Trick Tips: Sleigh Bells Ring**
You may want to use a set of sleigh bells for this trick; four or five bells on a long strap may make it easier for your dog to learn to ring a bell, because it will give her more opportunities to be right.

The shaping steps for teaching your dog to Ring a Bell are as follows:

**1.** Put the bells on the floor and click and treat your dog for sniffing them (you can use a Touch command if she knows one).
**2.** Delay the click and wait for her to touch harder or mouth them before you click and treat.
**3.** Work at this until she's ringing the bells with purpose.
**4.** Hang the bells next to the door and repeat the above steps until she is ringing them reliably.
**5.** Gradually increase the distance she must travel to touch the bells.
**6.** Verbally label ringing the bells, Bells.

## Dancing Dog

This trick is adorable but difficult for most dogs. To perform this trick the dog must balance on his hind legs and walk. You'll want to practice in short sessions to help your dog build up his back and leg muscles gradually. Be sure to work on a nonskid surface so that your dog does not injure himself. The shaping steps for teaching Dancing Dog are as follows:

1. With your dog in a Sit, hold your hand slightly above his nose and click and treat any effort to raise himself up on his back legs to touch your hand.
2. Raise your hand higher and continue to click and treat your dog for using his hind end to raise himself up and touch your hand.
3. Get your dog to hold the position longer by delaying the click by a second or two.
4. Gradually increase the time to several seconds.
5. Move your hand around and click and treat him for walking on his hind legs to touch it.
6. Turn your hand in a circle and click and treat your dog for walking on his hind legs to follow it.
7. Add the cue Dance by saying it just before the dog starts the behavior.

## Get Me a Bottle of Water

This amazing trick involves your dog opening the refrigerator, taking out a bottle of water, closing the door, and bringing the bottle of water to you. You'll probably want to start with a water bottle and then as your dog refines her techniques, you can change the water bottle to a can of soda or a bottle of juice. This trick has three different parts: retrieving the bottle, opening the refrigerator door, and closing the refrigerator door.

### Getting the Water Bottle
1. Hand your dog a bottle of water and tell her to Take It. Click and treat your dog for hanging on to it for several seconds at a time.
2. Move away from your dog and have her come to you over greater and greater distances. Click and treat her first as she is moving to you, and then for delivering the bottle to your hand.

3. Place the bottle on the floor and tell your dog to Take It, then Bring It. Click and treat her for retrieving it, then gradually withhold the click until the dog is on her way back to you.

4. Put the bottle on a low shelf of the refrigerator and practice having the dog Take It. Click and treat your dog for at first approaching, then taking, then bringing the bottle to you over short training sessions.

### Quick Fix: Use an Empty Can

Water bottles are the easiest for the dog to grasp at first, and later you can work up to retrieving cans or glass. If you have a dog who tends to bite down hard when he retrieves things, you may want to practice with empty cans first to prevent him from scaring himself or making a mess of your kitchen.

## Opening the Refrigerator Door

1. Put a strap on the refrigerator door to make it easier for your dog to open it.

2. Starting with the refrigerator door open, hand your dog the strap and tell him to Take It. Click and treat him for taking the strap.

3. Once your dog is taking the strap easily, delay the click for an extra second or two and click and treat your dog for holding it.

4. Standing slightly behind your dog, call him back to you while he holds the strap. You may need to go back and teach your dog the formal retrieve (see Chapter 8) with the strap or at least review it with him.

5. When he can hold on to the strap while backing up, click and treat him for actually moving the door.

6. Gradually close the door until it's almost clicked shut, so that your dog has to pull harder to open it.

7. Once your dog can open it when it's shut all the way, try letting him retrieve the strap on his own. At first, click and treat any attempt to take the strap.

8. Gradually add a little distance so that your dog is approaching the refrigerator from greater and greater distances.

9. Eventually delay your click so that your dog is taking the strap and starting to back up to pull the door open before you click. If at any time he seems confused and the behavior falls apart, go back and break things down into smaller parts and gradually rebuild the behavior.

### Closing the Door Using His Nose

1. Once your dog is comfortable holding the bottle in his mouth, practice having him target the refrigerator door with his nose.

2. Open the door a little, give a Touch command, and click and treat him for moving the door shut even a little.

3. Gradually leave the door open a little more until the dog is shutting the door with purpose. Make sure you click and treat your dog even for small attempts to push the door shut.

4. Verbally label the behavior Shut the Door.

### Closing the Door Using His Paws

An alternate option would be to have your dog use his paws on the refrigerator to close it.

1. Use a paw target to get him to touch the refrigerator with his paws, then click and treat.

2. Open the door a little and tell your dog to paw the door; click and treat him for moving the door shut.

3. Gradually open the door more so your dog has to push the door harder to earn the click and treat.

4. Verbally label the behavior Shut the Door.

Review each piece before putting them all together. Open the refrigerator door (keep the bottle on the lower shelf), and have your dog take the bottle. When he still has the bottle in his mouth, call him

ﻟe door and tell him to push it shut. Practice these two steps ᴜᴨᴛᴎ they are fluid. Then add the command to Take It (the door strap), followed by retrieving the bottle. Practice these together until they are fluid. Then, combine them with closing the door. You may have to go back and forth a bit in order to keep each part of the behavior strong until eventually it is one continuous behavior.

## Go Left, Go Right

Teaching your dog how to distinguish from his left and right will amaze your friends and family. It will also enable you to direct your dog to exactly where you want her to go.

1.  Start with your dog in front of an object (like a chair or a hassock) and put a target lid to the left of it about three feet away.
2.  Send your dog to go Touch, and click and treat her for responding.
3.  Repeat this at gradually increasing distances, clicking right before your dog touches her nose to the target.
4.  When your dog is offering the behavior readily, say the new cue Go Left just before she is about to move forward to touch the target. Repeat this until she will go to the left when you say left.
5.  Fade the target by making it smaller (use scissors to cut it into smaller pieces) until your dog simply moves left on command.
6.  To teach your dog to go right, simply follow all the same steps except with everything on the right.

You can combine the Go Left and Go Right commands with retrieving tricks by lining up several objects in a row and asking your dog to take the one on the left or the right. If nothing else, this trick will give you a better foundation for teaching your dog more complicated tricks.

## Find It

Sending your dog to find something you have lost is useful and exciting to the dog. Losing your wallet or keys in a pile of leaves or along your walking route could be disastrous—unless your dog can help in the search.

**1.** Choose an item with lots of your scent on it (like a hat or a hair tie) and show it to your dog.
**2.** Have someone hold your dog's collar while you hide the item somewhere obvious at first.
**3.** Release your dog to go find it and click and treat him as he approaches it.
**4.** Gradually increase the difficulty by hiding it in more challenging places.
**5.** Find another item to practice with and try again.
**6.** Label the behavior Find It as the dog moves toward the object.

# Chapter 10

# Family and Multi-Dog Tricks

As your dog's handler, you are her connection to the human world. If your dog is part of a larger family, however, each member of the family needs to have a good working relationship with your dog. Start training your dog as an active participant in family life, and everyone will benefit from it. When you and your dog are ready to get the whole family in on the action—and even include some other doggie playmates, too—these are the tricks for you.

## Go Wake Up Daddy

What better way to wake up each morning than with a canine alarm clock? This trick involves your dog giving a kiss or a nudge to the person she's waking up. To teach this, you'll need a helper to act as the person the dog is supposed to rouse.

**1.** Start with the helper lying face down with his head on his folded arms. Have your helper hide a handful of lures under his arm and encourage your dog to investigate. When your dog goes to stick her nose under the helper's arm, click and treat.

**2.** Fade the lures in the helper's hand until the dog is nudging the person without the food being present. Click and treat any attempt to burrow under the person's arm.

**3.** Label the behavior Wake Up and add the person's name just before the dog burrows under the person's arm.

**4.** Build your dog up to gradually increasing distances, until she is eagerly performing Wake Up from a room or two away.

**5.** Change helpers so that each member of the family gets a turn to be awakened by the dog.

**6.** Practice every Saturday morning to make sure no one misses out on breakfast!

### Trick Tips: Just Holler

As your dog begins to understand the concept of waking someone up, you can start to teach her to wake up specific people by having the person call her after you give the Wake Up command. Then, you can wean your dog off of this once she begins to catch on.

## Go Get Mommy

What better way to round up the family for dinnertime then to send the dog to bring each member to the table? This is a useful trick for kids and parents alike; for this trick the dog must go to a family member and lead them back to the person who sent them.

**1.** Using the person your dog is going to get as your helper, call the dog back and forth between you and click and treat him for going to each person.

**2.** When your dog is doing this enthusiastically, label the behavior Go and the person's name, right before the person calls the dog to Come.

3. Gradually move the people further apart so that the dog is going to the person from different rooms and up and down the stairs.

4. Replace the Come command with Go by saying Go Get and adding the person's name right before the person calls the dog to come. The person the dog is searching for should be doing the clicking and treating when the dog finds her.

5. Once the dog begins to offer the behavior readily, he can be weaned off the clicker and treats, but he should still be acknowledged with praise and affection.

## Pull Off My Socks

This is a wonderful trick for anyone who has trouble pulling off their own socks, or for moms hoping to speed up the undressing process while trying to herd the kids into the tub.

### Trick Tips: Try This with Old Socks First

You may want to start this trick with an old pair of socks. Dogs who love retrieving will find this trick particularly exciting, and they'll tend to rip a pair or two before they are able to perfect their technique!

Here are the shaping steps for teaching Pull Off My Socks:

1. Place an old sock on the floor and tell your dog to Take It.
2. Hold the ankle part of the sock, and shape your dog to take it by the toe.
3. Repeat until he is reliably taking the sock by the toe.
4. Add some resistance, and pull back gently when he takes the toe.
5. Delay the click until your dog is holding and pulling slightly for a second or two.
6. Gradually delay the click until he is hanging on and tugging back.
7. Put the sock on your foot so that most of it is hanging off, and start from the top.

8. Gradually delay the click until your dog is pulling the sock off your foot.

9. Gradually pull the sock further up your foot until it's almost all the way on.

10. Label the behavior Pull My Sock when it is happening reliably.

When teaching this behavior, use an adult as the sock wearer until your dog learns to use his mouth gently and not nibble your toes. Once your dog is a pro, you can gradually introduce new people, though you should always supervise young children.

### Tip Tricks: Making Multi-Dog Tricks Work

Successful multi-dog tricks require that each dog understands the behavior and can perform it on a reliable cue. Before attempting it with more than one dog, go over the steps with each dog individually. If things fall apart or don't go as well as planned, review the steps with each dog separately.

## Double-Dog Roll Over

This trick involves two dogs rolling over at the same time. As you position the dogs, make sure that you leave enough space in between them so that they don't crash into each other.

You can also have the dogs roll over one at a time, one right after the other. Shaping steps for the Double-Dog Roll Over are as follows:

1. Have each dog lie about three feet apart (allow more space if the dogs are giant breeds).

2. Reinforce each dog for holding the Down/Stay position.

3. Cue the dogs to Roll Over one at a time (reinforce the others for staying until they have been cued), or give the cue for all the dogs to roll at the same time.

4. Experiment with giving a cue to each dog and then giving one cue to the group to see which version of the trick looks flashier.
5. If you are cueing all the dogs at once, you need only one click for all of them, but treat each dog with her own cookie.
6. If you are cueing each dog separately, click and treat that dog before asking the next one to go.
7. Once the dogs are performing reliably, verbally label the behavior Everybody Over, or label each individual rollover with the dog's name and then the Roll Over command.

Trick Tips: Congenial Canines
If you are going to train multiple dogs to work together, it's a good idea to make sure they get along well and are not competitive over food.

## Pass the Cookie Please

This trick requires two dogs, one sitting in front of the other. The first dog balances a cookie on his nose and on cue, tosses his head back, flinging the cookie over his head to the dog sitting behind him. The dog sitting behind him catches it and eats it as his reward.

Shaping steps for teaching the first dog to balance a cookie on his nose are as follows:

1. Choose a flat cookie to help the dog learn to balance it.
2. Hold your dog's muzzle still and click and treat him for allowing you to do this.
3. Place a dog biscuit on the flat part of the top of his muzzle and click and treat him for holding his head still.
4. Use a Stay command and frequent clicks and treats to help your dog learn to balance the cookie on his nose.
5. Once he's got the balancing part, you can click after a certain number of seconds and release him to flip the cookie off his nose.

Add the second dog to the mix once your cookie-balancing dog has a good toss and is no longer immediately pursuing the dropped cookie. Practice having the second dog catch the cookie after the first dog tosses it. It may require lots of practice to get the timing and coordination just right. The commands or labels will be Hold It, Stay, and then Okay, This will cause the dog holding the cookie to toss the cookie, and the dog behind him will catch it. Be sure you click and treat the first dog for not pursuing the tossed cookie.

### Quick Fix: Helpers to Handle Multiple Dogs

Since two or three dogs are meant to perform these tricks at once, handling them all yourself might get tricky. If so, enlist the help of multiple handlers, one for each dog. The helpers can reinforce and reward individual dogs for performing correctly while they get used to performing tricks as a team.

## Everybody Wave

This adorable trick can be performed with any number of dogs. The dogs should line up facing their audience and raise a paw in the air as if waving hello. The shaping steps for teaching a group of dogs to wave are as follows:

1. Make sure each dog can fluently and reliably wave on a hand signal.
2. Line the dogs up and reinforce them for holding a Stay.
3. Cue the dogs to Wave and click and treat all of them.
4. Practice with two dogs at a time until they are competing with each other to raise their paws the fastest.
5. Encourage extra-fast efforts by clicking and treating only the dog that was first.
6. Gradually add more dogs, following the same rules; the faster dogs get treated more often than the slower dogs.

**7.** If one dog is particularly slow, take him aside and teach him to wave faster before putting him back into the group.

### Trick Tips: Use This Trick When Visiting

This trick is an adorable way to say hello or good-bye during a visit with school children or a visit at a nursing home. You can vary how the dogs perform the trick by having them wave individually or as a group.

You can improve on each dog's individual wave by only clicking and treating the best versions of the wave, one aspect at a time. For instance, you might improve the speed of the dog's response by giving the cue and only clicking and treating when he offers the behavior within a certain amount of time (say three seconds). You might improve the height of the wave by only clicking and treating the higher waves and ignoring the lower ones, telling the dog to try again. Just be sure that you are concentrating on one aspect at a time so as not to confuse the dog.

## Leap Frog

Be careful which dogs you choose for this trick; not all dogs are comfortable having other dogs jump over them. This trick requires two to three dogs. While the rest of the dogs lie down about three feet apart, the third dog leaps over their backs and lies down next to the first dog. The second dog, who is now the first dog, then repeats this, and so on.

**1.** Reinforce all the dogs for lying down and holding the Stay.
**2.** Work the third dog by having her touch her nose to the target stick held over the back of the second dog. Use the target stick to help her hop over the other dogs one at a time; click and treat each hop.
**3.** When the last dog has been hopped over, have the new first dog lie down and let the next dog go.

4. Reinforce the other dogs for holding the Down/Stay position. You may need a helper for this.

5. Adding speed to this trick will make it impressive and flashy; just be sure to build up to it slowly and don't rush the dogs. When they are comfortable they will move faster.

### Quick Fix: Practice the Hop Over

If your dog has a hard time tolerating other dogs hopping over her, practice by stepping over her, and reinforce her when she cooperates.

## Take a Bow

For this trick the dog brings his front end close to the ground, with his chest resting on the floor, lifts his tail end in the air, and holds the position. You can have the dogs do all of these things at the same time or one after the other.

Lab Mix and Golden Retriever bow together

1.  It's probably best to start with all the dogs in the Sit/Stay position. Reinforce each dog for holding the Stay.
2.  Give the cue for Bow to all the dogs at once, or each dog individually. Click and treat those dogs that perform the behavior correctly.
3.  Continue to practice until all the dogs are performing in unison. Don't be afraid to go back and review the steps with each dog individually if the trick starts to fall apart. (See Chapter 7 to review the shaping steps for teaching your dog to bow.)

## Walking the Dog

This trick involves two dogs. One dog wears a collar and leash and the other dog carries the leash in her mouth.

1.  Teach your dog to retrieve and carry a leash. (See Chapter 8 for shaping the retrieve behavior.)
2.  Once your dog is retrieving the leash easily, practice having her hold it with some resistance (hold on to the end and give a little tug).
3.  Hand your dog the leash and click and treat her for grabbing it and walking with you.
4.  With the leash firmly in your dog's mouth, practice giving it a tug, and click and treat her for pulling back or hanging on.
5.  Gradually increase the amount of resistance you offer to prepare her for a real dog on the end of the lead.
6.  When she can carry the leash while you are offering resistance, go ahead and add a real dog.
7.  The dog you add should be an adult with some leash manners, and the leash should be attached to a flat buckled collar.
8.  The dog being led should be clicked and treated for walking slightly ahead of the other dog but not outright pulling.

## Tips for Great Performances

When working with multiple dogs it quickly becomes apparent that the better able the dogs are to perform the tricks alone, the more likely they are to cooperate as a group. There are some tricks to working with groups of dogs who understand what is expected but need to learn how to do the behavior in unison.

- Only treat those dogs who perform the trick fast.
- Point to the individual dog that you are working with as you give the cue.
- Use a helper to reward the other dogs for holding a Stay while you work with an individual dog.
- Review tricks regularly with each individual dog to keep performance consistent.
- Vary the quality and quantity of treats to keep your dog guessing and trying harder to earn the next goodie.
- Keep your sessions short and frequent to keep the dogs focused and sharp.

### Quick Fix: Reward Waiting Dogs

It can't be stressed enough that if you don't reward the dogs who are waiting their turn to perform, you will lose their interest. Rewarding these dogs will ensure that all the dogs stay focused and ready to work.

The showoff in every dog is something to celebrate! Enjoy spending time teaching your dog tricks and performing them for friends and family, and let your dog—or dogs—indulge their sense of humor and excitement by making them part of your entertainment committee.

## Chapter 11

# Center Stage

If your dog masters a variety of tricks for fun at home, it might be time to think about getting involved in advanced dog-sport events. There are many different types of dog sports (both competitive and noncompetitive) that you and your pooch can participate in, and it's not difficult to find classes for all of these activities. Ask your trainer if he or she offers such classes, contact your local breed club, check the offerings at your local community college, or search the Internet.

Before you sign up for a class in a particular dog sport, be sure your dog is ready to perform. As is true in the case of all the tricks described up to this point, your dog must know and respond to basic obedience commands in order to participate in these sports. If you have to call him several times before he comes or if he won't sit or lie down the first time you tell him to do so, a little remedial work at home or in a class is in order before trying a dog sport.

## An Overview of Events

The American Kennel Club sanctions a variety of events that will keep you and your dog young and healthy for many years to come. Sometimes, these performance events are very general in their competition; other times, they are breed- or group-specific. The AKC events are for purebred dogs only, but other organizations allow any breed or mixed breed to compete.

All of these events are a lot of fun to compete in but if true competition isn't for you, perhaps you can find a club or training facility that offers regular practice matches for you to participate in. The following are just some of the organized events that you can participate in:

*Obedience Trials*                     *Herding*
*Agility Trials*                       *Lure Coursing*
*Tracking*                             *Earthdog Tests*
*Field Trials and Hunting Tests*

### What about Mixed Breeds?

Don't worry if your dog is not purebred. There are other organizations besides the AKC that sponsor different competitive events. Mixed breeds are eligible to compete in agility trials sponsored by Canine Performance Events, USDAA, and NADAC, for instance. If you find that your mixed-breed dog has a talent for a particular sport, do some research and find out if there are any sponsored events for that activity in your area. The following sections provide a brief overview of sporting events for dogs, many of which incorporate performing fun and interesting tricks. So if you and your dog are ready to take center stage and strut your stuff in public, read on!

## Obedience Trials

The idea of obedience is to help meld you and your dog into a good working team. Obedience Trialing is a rewarding endeavor that doesn't require extensive travel or a lot of money investment. Anyone can participate in the sport of dog obedience—desire is far more important than natural talent. People of all ages and physical conditions can become top competitors, and dogs of all breeds and backgrounds (rescued and formerly abused dogs, too) appear in the winner's circle. Handlers who participate in obedience training will experience the rewards of a better-trained dog as well as the camaraderie with peers—and maybe even the thrill of earning an occasional title.

Obedience trials test and score a dog's ability to perform specific exercises. The American Kennel Club sanctions the majority of these events. The AKC has more than 13,000 field trial, obedience, and other specialty clubs, and hundreds of AKC-sanctioned dog shows occur every week all over the United States. Trials governed by the United Kennel Club, States Kennel Club, and others are also quickly gaining popularity. Regardless of which kennel club is governing, the rules are nearly identical, or involve only minor variations, so little additional training is required to earn more titles. In AKC and most other obedience competitions, dogs work toward titles in three levels, each progressively more difficult. The classes, titles, and general summary of requirements are as follows:

**Novice—Companion Dog (CD):** This level includes on- and off-leash heeling, recall and stand, sit and down stay. Novice is the only class in which the dog is leashed for part of the performance and, when the leash is removed, the handler can guide the dog by the collar while moving from one exercise to the next.

**Open—Companion Dog Excellent (CDX):** This level involves commands such as drop on recall, retrieve on flat, retrieve over high jump, broad jump, and sit and down stays with the handlers out of sight.

**Utility—Utility Dog (UD):** This category tests hand signals, scent discrimination, moving stand, and directed jumping and retrieving.

Open and Utility are considered the advanced classes. In these, the leash is removed as the team enters the ring. The dog is never touched, except to be measured or praised. In order to earn a title in each level the dog must earn three qualifying scores. A perfect score is 200 points, and to qualify a dog must earn 170 points and 50 percent of the available points for each exercise.

Dogs who earn a UD are eligible to compete for two other obedience titles. The UDX (Utility Dog Excellent) is earned when the dog qualifies in Open and Utility class at the same show ten times. After a dog accumulates one hundred points, he wins the OTCh (Obedience Trial Championship). A dog earns points if he places first or second in Open or Utility, and the size of the class determines the number of points earned.

### Trick Tips: Learning More about Obedience Trials

For information about Obedience Trials, check out The American Kennel Club Web site, at **www.akc.org**, or the United Kennel Club Web site, at **www.ukcdogs.com**. You're likely to find events several times each month that take place within easy driving distance from where you live.

This is the only competitive obedience title, meaning a dog earns points by defeating other dogs, rather than simply performing exercises in accordance with the rulebook. Special competitions, otherwise known as tournaments, are held for the best of the best. In order to enter, the dog must prove himself at AKC or other kennel-club sanctioned events. Top obedience dogs are ranked each year using various systems designed by breed clubs, obedience clubs, and obedience publications such as *Front and Finish*, or *The Dog Trainer's News*. Although these aren't official designations, they're esteemed and sought after.

American Kennel Club competitions are limited to purebred registered and ILP (indefinite listing privilege) dogs, but many other governing bodies allow mixed breeds to compete. All obedience competitions allow spayed and neutered dogs to participate. If you'd like to observe an Obedience Trial, call local training clubs (listed in the Yellow Pages) or browse dog show superintendents' pages on the Internet.

## Agility Trials

This fun, fast-paced sport stresses teamwork, expert training, and athleticism. Agility requires the dog—directed by his handler—to navigate a series of obstacles, such as A-frames, balance beams, tunnels, and weave poles, as well as different types of jumps—through tires, hoops, or over single or double bars, for instance.

In Agility Trials, classes are divided by jump heights determined by the dog's height at the shoulder. The judge determines the order of the obstacles, and handlers are allowed to walk the course for ten minutes prior to the beginning of their class (without their dogs) to plan their strategy. This is a timed event where the dog and handler must complete the course in order within the predetermined amount of time in order to receive a qualifying score. Point deductions in the form of wrong courses and faults are deducted from a total score of 100. Each level allows a certain number of faults and wrong courses to the handler and dog; the higher the level the more perfect the performance must be. In AKC Agility, there are four levels of competition:

*Novice Agility* (the title you earn is NA)
*Open Agility* (the title you earn is OA)
*Agility Excellent* (the title you earn is AX)
*Master Agility Excellent* (the title you earn is MX)

Recently, the AKC has added another category called Preferred for dogs who are unable to jump their full height due to age or their owners' preference. Dogs competing in this performance class jump in the next lower category for their height. The letter P comes after each of their titles; NAP is novice agility preferred.

Welsh Terrier jumping
through a hoop

In order to earn a title, your dog must attain three qualifying scores, referred to as legs. Top score is 100 points, dogs are judged on speed and accuracy, and infractions are deducted from 100. First through fourth place is awarded to dogs who have the highest scores by their course times.

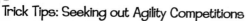

### Trick Tips: Seeking out Agility Competitions

If you're interested in agility, check out organizations such as American Kennel Club, the United States Dog Agility Association, the North American Dog Agility Council, and the United Kennel Club. They all sponsor Agility competitions. (Titles and rules vary from organization to organization.)

Dogs who enjoy being athletic and have a strong learning ability and a willingness to please make good Agility prospects. If your dog has the ability to think for himself but also takes direction well, that's a plus in this sport, too. Even if your dog doesn't have the speed of top Agility breeds, such as the Border collie, he can still be capable of solid, consistent Agility performance.

Before starting Agility training, your dog should know and respond to basic commands including Sit, Down, Stay, and Come. Even young puppies can begin to learn elements of agility, such as going through tunnels, balancing on the teeter-totter, and negotiating the A-frame set at a low height. You should avoid teaching your puppy to jump higher than elbow height (theirs, not yours) until they reach physical maturity at eighteen months of age.

### Trick Tips: Do a Health Check

As with any sport, a dog who competes in Agility must be in excellent physical condition. Take your dog in for a veterinary exam before beginning training. Health conditions such as hip dysplasia or other musculoskeletal problems, decreased vision, heart problems, and obesity preclude participation in agility.

Agility is fast becoming one of the most popular of all dog sports, because it's tremendous fun. It's always an exceptional show, so you and your dog are sure to be entertained whether you decide to compete or not!

## Tracking

Tracking requires not just a good nose, but an understanding of what is required in what can be a serious profession. Teach your dog to track, and you'll have a dog with a useful skill, as well as a new way to enjoy the outdoors with him. Your dog can earn an AKC tracking title by completing a single successful track.

By following a human scent trail, dogs can earn several titles:

*Tracking Dog* (TD)
*Tracking Dog Excellent* (TDX)
*Variable Surface Tracking* (VST)

For the TD test, the track is 440 to 500 yards long, with a minimum of two right-angle turns. It must be half an hour to two hours old. The person laying the track must be unfamiliar to the dog. At the end of the track, the person laying the track drops a scent article, which the dog must locate. The TDX track is longer, older (three to five hours), more complicated, and includes more varied terrain, such as ditches, streambeds, and tall grass. Its length is 800 to 1,000 yards, and it has several turns and two cross tracks. Along the way, there are also dummy scent articles meant to lure your dog off the trail.

TD and TDX tests usually take place in rural areas, but the VST tests a dog's tracking ability in more developed locales, such as suburban neighborhoods or city streets. The length of a VST track is 600 to 800 yards, and it goes over at least three types of surfaces, such as asphalt, concrete, grass, gravel, or sand. To add to the difficulty, a portion of the track must lack vegetation, which helps to hold scent. The track must be three to five hours old with four to eight turns. A dog who passes all three tests earns the title champion tracker (CT).

This competition is open to all breeds, and it's surprising how many breeds participate. Although many people work at tracking with their dogs just as a hobby, some dogs who start out in this competition go on to search-and-rescue or police work.

## Fieldwork

Field Trials and Hunting Tests are performance events that individual dog clubs sponsor. They are held under AKC rules and regulations but are put on by the sponsoring club. This means that they are always in the market for volunteers to help them run a smooth trial. If this is an area of interest to you and you'd like to find out more, offer to help at a trial to see what it's like.

Field Trials and Hunting Tests are performance events aimed at the Sporting group (and a few hounds). These events evaluate a dog's ability to retrieve game (the function for which some dogs, such as Golden and Labrador Retrievers, were originally bred). Field-work is a great opportunity for these sorts of breeds that have natural retrieving tendencies to show their abilities and earn titles. This sport involves retrieving lots of fallen birds, some of which are already dead (thrown by helpers to simulate being shot). Puppies who show retrieving instinct early can be introduced to birds as soon as eight to nine weeks of age. Teaching your dog to retrieve fallen birds requires that your dog have a basic knowledge of the retrieve. As always, a dog should also be familiar with basic commands. Commands such as Sit, Down, Stay, Heel, and Come form the foundation for hunting training. A dog should also be trained to remain quiet until given further instructions, because barking and whining are penalized and can even cause a dog to be eliminated from the stake.

Field-trial preparation also involves conditioning, to make sure a dog is in good shape for the amount of work he'll be doing. If you're interested in Field Trials, you should work your dog gradually until he's able to walk or run for several miles a day.

## Trick Tips: Know the Environment

If you're serious about this competition, your dog needs to be familiar with environments similar to those at a Field Trial. Take him for walks in woods, fields, and parks so he becomes accustomed to different types of foliage, the sounds of snapping twigs and crunching leaves, and the presence of many different smells.

When teaching your dog to do fieldwork, keep in mind that it's a bad idea to let his first experience with retrieving be something that's a dead, smelly bird that he would much rather roll on than put in his mouth. You might start with a bumper (a cylindrical plastic or canvas training aid) or a plastic model of a dead duck. The benefit to this is that you don't have to keep thawing out and re-freezing dead birds, which tend to smell quite ripe after a while. Using the shaping steps for retrieving already described in Chapter 8, choose one of these objects as your starter. When your dog is willingly picking up and holding the bumper or plastic bird dummy, switch it for the real thing and start again.

Once your dog learns how to retrieve the bird, it's then your job to think up as many circumstances as possible that he will encounter in his field career. The birds he's supposed to retrieve might be hidden in tall grass or in bushes. Sometimes they will be waterlogged and hardly breaking the water surface. Your dog will have to retrieve in all kinds of weather and despite distractions like birds flying overhead, gunshots, or other working dogs. Teach him to pick up the bird under as many of these circumstances as you can.

### Field-Trial Specifics

A good retriever is able to follow the trajectory of a shot bird and find where it landed. He isn't afraid to go after a bird, no matter where it is, and he retrieves with style. He pays attention to his handler, has a good sense of smell, and doesn't shy away from the sound of gunfire. Retrievers should perform equally well on land and in water. Just as important, a good retriever has a soft mouth, meaning he doesn't damage the bird during the retrieve. Retrievers are judged on their ability to mark, or remember, the location of downed birds, retrieve them quickly, and then deliver them gently to their handlers.

Dogs compete against each other for placements and points toward a field championship. The titles that can be earned are:

*Amateur Field Champion* (AFC)
*Field Champion* (FC)

Once earned, these titles become part of the dog's name. For instance, a dog with a field championship would have a registered name that looks like this: FC King Buck.

To participate, dogs must be at least six months old and registered with the AKC. Field Trial classes, known as stakes, test dogs of varying ages and levels of experience. Stakes also separate amateur and professional handlers. Retriever Field Trials have four stakes, two major and two minor. The major stakes are classified as open all-age and amateur all-age; the minor stakes are classified as qualifying and derby. Championship points are earned in the two major stakes, with at least two judges officiating.

### Trick Tips: Field Trial Eliminations

Be sure your dog is prepared for just about anything in this sport. Dogs can be eliminated from trials for such behaviors as failure to enter rough cover, water, ice, mud, or any other unpleasant or difficult situation; returning to the handler before finding a bird in a marked retrieve; stopping the hunt; repeated evidence of poor scenting ability; or failing to pick a bird up after finding it.

## Hunt-Test Specifics

Hunting Tests are a means of judging a dog's ability to perform against a standard of perfection established by the AKC regulations. Unlike Field Trials, they are noncompetitive, meaning the dogs must simply meet a standard of performance, rather than beat other dogs. Dogs who receive qualifying scores at a given number of tests can earn the following titles:

*Junior Hunter* (JH)
*Senior Hunter* (SH)
*Master Hunter* (MH)

Each successive title requires more skill, and dogs are judged more strictly as they advance. Once a dog has qualified at a higher level, she cannot move back to a lower level.

Beginners start with marked birds, meaning they can see the bird or bumper fly and fall. They must then stay until the handler gives the command to retrieve the bird. As the dog advances, Hunting Tests become more difficult, but at all levels the dog is usually not required to retrieve from a distance greater than 100 yards.

If you're interested in getting started with Hunting Tests, join a local club. By training with a group, you'll benefit from the experiences of other people and learn a variety of training techniques.

## Herding

Not surprisingly, Herding is aimed at the Herding group. The relationship with herding dogs is one of the oldest relationships humans have. Herding-Trial exercises are used to gauge the development of what is still a very important job for many herding dogs. Although Herding is more about doing work than performing tricks, it's included here because it's also a lot of fun. The AKC separates herding dogs into four distinct groups:

**Shepherd:** These dogs are usually used with sheep and typically lead a flock.

**Drover:** These dogs work livestock from behind, usually sheep or cattle.

**Livestock Guarding:** These dogs don't move livestock; they guard it from other predators.

**All-Round Farm Dogs:** These dogs usually can respond quickly to different situations and can perform a number of different jobs.

The first few exercises are called tests. These test the general inborn instincts of your animal and his ability to be trained. After that, you're off to the pasture. There are six different levels to achieve. The first two tests are:

*Herding Tested* (HT)
*Pre-Trail Tested* (PT)

In these levels, your dog's abilities are judged, again, based on inborn reaction as well as certain trained functions. The next levels are progressively harder. The idea is that a dog must keep ducks, sheep, or cattle together, sometimes under very difficult circumstances. The four remaining certificates to be achieved are:

*Herding Started* (HS)
*Herding Intermediate* (HI)
*Herding Excellent* (HX)
*Herding Champion* (HCh)

## Lure Coursing

Lure Coursing is mainly for Sight Hounds (dogs that hunt by sight), and it's probably one of the best spectator sports in all of dogdom. Over an open, but rigged, course, sight hounds (used by humans to hunt over open plains since the time of the Pharaohs) chase a flag at incredibly fast speeds. The breeds of dogs involved include Afghan Hounds, Basenjis, Borzoi, Greyhounds, Ibiza Hounds, Rhodesian Ridgebacks, Salukis, Scottish Deerhounds, and Whippets. A lure, or prey (which in most cases is a fluttering plastic bag), is pulled quickly along a series of wires, as the dogs give chase. In Lure Coursing, dogs are judged on overall ability, quickness, endurance, follow, and agility. Three titles can be earned:

*Junior Courser*  (JC)
*Senior Courser*  (SC)
*Field Champion*  (FC)

## Earthdog Tests

Earthdog Tests are noncompetitive events designed to test the hunting skills of small breeds such as Terriers and Dachshunds. Dogs such as these, once called "ratters," were traditionally bred to help farmers kill rodents and other small mammals that damage crops, so it's no surprise that the entry-level test, called Introduction to Vermin, entails chasing mice. Here's how it works: Two large mice or rats are placed safely in a cage at the end of a long underground tunnel, and then the dog is let loose. The dog is judged on his desire to do everything necessary to get to those two rodents trapped in a cage underground. (Don't fret about the welfare of these furry little critters—the rodents are safe, as the dogs cannot actually get to them.)

Three Earthdog titles can be earned:

*Junior Earthdog*  (JE)
*Senior Earthdog*  (SE)
*Master Earthdog*  (ME)

If you have one of these small dogs, this could be a great event for her.

# Chapter 12

# Other Sports in the Great Outdoors

In case you're still looking for additional activities beyond the Trial Events described in the last chapter, there are plenty of other sports for you and your dog to try. Activities such as Flyball and Freestyle have national organizations (as listed in the Resources section) that can direct you to people in your area who participate in a given sport. Don't forget that many of these activities don't require dogs to be purebred—anyone can get involved!

## Rally Obedience

The relatively new sport of rally obedience, which borrows its name from the sport of road rally for cars, has gained in popularity in recent years. Charles "Bud" Kramer, a dog-sport enthusiast, designed the sport. Bud has been instrumental in using positive training methods with dogs in the sport of agility, and more recently he has applied those methods to rally obedience. He pitched rally to the AKC for review, and it's currently offered through the AKC as a non-obedience class at Obedience Trials. The AKC allows only purebred dogs to compete, but other organizations, such as the Association of Pet Dog Trainers (or APDT), allow both purebred and mixed dogs to compete.

Designed to test the dog-and-handler team's ability to work together, this sport is similar to competitive obedience without the formality. This is great news for people put off by the strictness of competitive obedience who still want to get out and have fun with their dogs. Courses are designed to test the handler and dog's ability to follow signs, which are spread out on the testing field.

## Trick Tips: Exploring Rally Obedience

If you're interested in learning more about this new sport, check out Rally Obedience online, at **www.rallyobedience.com**. The site offers a link to the AKC's Rally Obedience page, as well as a chart with an exercise list, brief descriptions, and images of the signs used for the sport.

The handler and dog must perform the exercises according to the rules, but the handler may talk to the dog, cue him with gestures, encourage him, and praise him. Unlike competitive obedience, where only one command is allowed, rally obedience actually encourages handlers to talk to and praise their dogs during performance. No food or toys are allowed on the course, as the course is designed to test the dog's level of competence at each level.

The course designer selects from forty-five different approved rally exercises and designs a course with about twenty-five to twenty-eight different exercises that the handler must perform successfully. As in agility competition, the handler is allowed to walk the course ahead of time to plan out a strategy. Seven of the rally exercises can be used more than once, but the rest cannot be repeated. Each directional sign gives instructions for a specific exercise. When the handler and dog complete it, they move on to the next exercise.

Golden Retriever
weaving through legs

## Sample Rally Exercises

Rally exercises are designed to demonstrate and test a dog's response to obedience, but with an element of fun. Here are some exercises you might find on a rally course:

- Figure eight
- 90-degree turn
- 180-degree turn
- 360-degree turn
- Halt: Stop, with dog sitting parallel
- Spirals: Circle cones while dog heels by doing the outside three, then two, then one.

## Judging Rally Obedience

There are currently two levels of rally performance, but more levels could easily be added with more complicated exercises.

**Level 1:** This is the entry level and is performed on leash.
**Level 2:** This level is performed off-leash and is more challenging.

Each dog-and-handler team starts with 200 points, and judges deduct points as the handler or dog make various errors. Point deductions range from one-half to three points. If a dog loses five or more points on one exercise, he cannot qualify. This might happen if a dog does not remain in a Stay, fails to Come on the recall, misses a jump, or knocks over a cone. In general, however, the dog's attitude, attention, and response are emphasized over his precision.

Rally obedience is extremely dog- and person-friendly, and it's a great sport to try whether your dog is young or old. Many clubs and groups offer matches for the fun of it, and handlers show up in great numbers to work their dogs for the same reason. The lack of intense competition makes this a more relaxed and fun sport, so if you're a hesitant competitor or a person who just wants to get out and enjoy being with your best friend, this might be a great sport for you to try.

## Flyball Competition

Flyball is an exciting, fast-action sport with great spectator appeal. The North American Flyball Association (or NAFA) organizes and oversees tournaments in North America. All dogs, both purebred and mixed breed, are eligible to compete. Even dogs who are not totally tennis-ball crazed can be taught using positive reinforcement to hit the box, grab the ball, and jump the jumps.

### How the Game Is Played

Flyball races consist of two relay teams, with four dogs on each team. Jumps are set to be four inches lower than the shoulder height of the shortest dog on the team. The minimum height is eight inches, while the maximum is sixteen inches. The hurdles are spaced about ten feet apart, with the handler standing behind the start line while the dog works. The first jump is six feet from the start/finish line, and the Flyball box is set a distance of fifteen feet from the last jump. The total length of the course is fifty-one feet.

The handler stands behind the start line and holds the dog by the collar. When the go is given, the handler releases the dog, who jumps over all four hurdles to the Flyball box. The dog must hit a pedal on the box to release the ball, catch the ball, and then turn around and race back over the same four jumps to the finish line. The next handler in line releases the next dog as the previous dog crosses the finish. If the dog loses the ball or misses a jump, he must run again after the remainder of the team has gone. The first team to finish without errors wins. This all happens in twenty seconds or less, with the winning team clinching victory by a split second. If you've got a trick-crazed canine who loves fast-paced activities, Flyball competition could be in order!

## Trick Tips: Risk of Injury

This fast-paced, fun sport is not without risk of injury. Jumping, bouncing off the box, and turning sharply on the return all take their toll on the dog's body. Depending upon the dog's level of fitness and physical shape, a handler can minimize injuries by practicing regularly and stopping the action if the dog seems out of control.

Flyball is hard on the body, and joints such as hocks, elbows, knees, and shoulders take a beating. Before getting started, take your dog to the veterinarian to be X-rayed for hip and elbow problems. Many serious competitors also X-ray shoulders, knees, and backs, just to be on the safe side. It's also a good idea to have your veterinarian check for eye problems.

## Flyball Awards and Titles

At NAFA-sanctioned events, teams are divided into different divisions so that they compete against teams of equal ability. This way, each team has a chance at winning an individual race. Dogs earn points toward Flyball titles by completing the race within a certain amount of time. The team does not have to win the race, only complete it.

Points are awarded by how quickly the race is run. If teams finish in less than thirty-two seconds, each dog on the team gets one point. If the team runs in less than twenty-eight seconds, each dog earns five points. If the team comes in under twenty-four seconds, each dog earns twenty-five points toward his title. Titles are awarded for varying point levels, from twenty all the way to 30,000 points.

The North American Flyball Association confers three different titles for this sport:

*Flyball Dog* (FD)
*Flyball Dog Excellent* (FDX)
*Flyball Dog Champion* (FbDCh)

## Trick Tips: Vary Exercise

Flyball should never be your dog's only exercise. It's important to build muscle and endurance in an athletic dog daily with varying activities such as swimming, off-leash play, walks up and down hills, and retrieving games.

Not all Flyball events are for competition, however. Some teams get together to run their dogs just for the fun of it or to give demonstrations at dog shows or other events.

The best way to get started with Flyball is to contact local trainers. Find out if anyone in your area offers a class or workshop, or if there is a local team you could practice with to learn about the sport. Try to find a team with a like-minded philosophy for training, as you will be working closely with them as you train your dog to compete.

## Dog Sledding

You'd think this one would only be popular in Alaska, right? Not a chance. More and more dog sledding clubs are starting up all over the United States and all over the world. Many Spitz breed fans have joined forces, and, with the help of new technologies (sleds on wheels) and a devotion to the sport, have brought about new ways to train and compete with dog-sled teams in areas not covered by snow and ice. And here's the *really* fun news: Other breeds are presently teaming up and competing as well.

The premiere guiding force in all of this is the International Sled Dog Racing Association, and it has branches all over the country. There are even some clubs as far south as Virginia and North Carolina!

## Schutzhund or Protection Events

Schutzhund is German for "protection dog." Today, different levels of Schutzhund training have been assigned to help qualify dogs for police work as well as for protection. This sport combines aspects of tracking, obedience, and protection. Schutzhund requires tremendous hours of training and requires a dog who is calm and self-assured. A hyper or anxious dog, one that lacks confidence or is easily distracted, is probably not a good candidate for Schutzhund. Although there are many people who are qualified for this type of training, the most notable dogs in this sport tend to be dogs used for police work.

## Freestyle

Nicknamed the tail-wagging sport, freestyle involves developing a routine set to music that highlights dog and handler working together, expressing their creativity through movement and costume. Routines can be based on obedience exercises, tricks, or any other behaviors the dog knows and enjoys. It's perfect for athletic, attentive, well-trained dogs.

There are two types of freestyle:

- *Heelwork to music:* This involves heeling on all sides of the handler, with the dog no farther away than 4 feet.
- *Musical freestyle:* This is an anything-goes routine that often encompasses jumping and fancy tricks.

Handlers select the beat that goes along with the dog's performance and choreograph moves based on their dogs' abilities. Dogs can start training for freestyle at any age, and even dogs with health issues can participate, because it's simple to adapt the choreography and music to suit a dog's speed and ability level.

## Ultimate Frisbee Tricks

You're probably thinking this one is easy to figure out—after all, lots of folks play Frisbee with their dogs all the time, right? Think again, because this is not your leisurely game of Frisbee in the back yard. This stuff is fast, furious, and wicked. Canine Frisbee competitions happen all over the country, and watching some of the top Frisbee dogs do their stunts and tricks, and compete against others, is as amazing as it gets.

Trick Tips: Finding out about Frisbee Competitions
If you're interested in finding out more about Frisbee trick competition, go to **www.dogpatch.org** and click on the Frisbee option. There, you'll find information and tips on Frisbee training, competition and event scheduling, equipment, and specific styles and tricks to teach your dog.

# Appendix

## Resources

### Books

Abrantes, Roger. *Dog Language: An Encyclopedia of Canine Behavior*. (Naperville, IL: Wakan Tanka Publishers, 1997).

Benjamin, Carol. *Dog Problems*. (New York, NY: Hungry Minds, Inc., 1989).

Burch, Mary R. and Jon S. Bailey. *How Dogs Learn* (New York, NY: Hungry Minds, Inc., 1999).

Campbell, William E. *Behavior Problems in Dogs*, Third Revised Edition (Grants Pass, OR: BehaviorRx Systems, 1999).

Campbell, William E. *Owner's Guide to Better Behavior in Dogs*. (Loveland, CO: Alpine Publishers, 1989).

Cantrell, Krista. *Catch Your Dog Doing Something Right: How to Train Any Dog in Five Minutes a Day* (New York, NY: Plume Publishers, 1998).

Donaldson, Jean. *The Culture Clash* (Berkeley, CA: James and Kenneth Publishing, 1997).

Donaldson, Jean. *Dogs Are from Neptune* (Montreal, Quebec: Lasar Multimedia Productions, 1998).

Dunbar, Ian. *Dr. Dunbar's Good Little Dog Book* (Berkeley, CA: James and Kenneth Publishers, 1992).

Dunbar, Ian. *How to Teach a New Dog Old Tricks* (Berkeley, CA: James and Kenneth Publishers, 1998).

Evans, Job Michael. *Training and Explaining: How to Be the Dog Trainer You Want to Be*. (New York, NY: Hungry Minds, Inc., 1995).

Fox, Dr. Michael W. *Understanding Your Dog.* (New York, NY: St. Martin's Press, 1972).

Milani, D.V.M., Myrna. *The Body Language and Emotions of Dogs.* (New York, NY: William Morrow and Company, 1986).

Milani, D.V.M., Myrna. *DogSmart.* (Chicago, IL: Contemporary Publishing, 1997).

Owens, Paul. *The Dog Whisperer: A Compassionate, Nonviolent Approach to Dog Training* (Avon, MA: Adams Media, 1999).

Pryor, Karen. *Don't Shoot the Dog: The New Art of Teaching and Training*, Revised Edition (New York, NY: Bantam Books, 1999).

Pryor, Karen. *Karen Pryor on Behavior: Essays and Research.* (North Bend, WA: Sunshine Books, 1994).

Reid, Ph.D., Pamela. *Excel-Erated Learning: Explaining in Plain English How Dogs Learn and How Best to Teach Them.* (Oakland, CA: James and Kenneth Publishers, 1996).

Rugaas, Turid. *On Talking Terms with Dogs: Calming Signals* (Carlsborg, WA: Legacy By Mail, 1997).

Ryan, Terry. *The Toolbox for Remodeling Your Problem Dog* (New York, NY: Howell Book House, 1998).

Schwartz, Charlotte. *The Howell Book of Puppy Raising.* (New York, NY: Hungry Minds, Inc., 1987).

Scott, John Paul and John L. Fuller. *Genetics and the Social Behavior of the Dog.* (Chicago, IL: University of Chicago Press, 1965).

Tellington-Jones, Linda. *Getting in Touch with Your Dog: A Gentle Approach to Influencing Health, Behavior, and Performance* (Pomfret, VT: Trafalgar Square, 2001).

Wilkes, Gary. *A Behavior Sampler* (North Bend, WA: Sunshine Books, 1994).

## Videos

Broitman, Virginia. *Bow Wow, Take 2* (Littleton, CO: Canine Training Systems, 1996).

Broitman, Virginia and Sherry Lippman. *Take a Bow Wow* (Littleton, CO: Canine Training Systems, 1996).

Jones, Deborah. *Click & Fetch* (Littleton, CO: Canine Training Systems, 1999).

Pryor, Karen. *Clicker Magic! The Art of Clicker Training* (North Bend, WA: Sunshine Books, 1997).

Pryor, Karen. *Puppy Love* (North Bend, WA: Sunshine Books, 1999).

Rugaas, Turid. *Calming Signals: What Your Dog Tells You* (Carlsborg, WA: Legacy By Mail, 2001).

Wilkes, Gary. *Click! & Treat Training Kit* (Phoenix, AZ: Click! & Treat Products, 1996).

Wilkes, Gary. *The Doggie Repair Kit* (Phoenix, AZ: Click! & Treat Products, 1996).

## Web Sites

Canine University®: *www.canineuniversity.com*

Clicker Teachers Listing: *www.clickerteachers.net*

DogWise: *www.dogwise.com*

Karen Pryor's Web site: *www.dontshootthedog.com*

William Campbell's Web site: *www.webtrail.com/petbehavior/index.html*

## Organizations
**American Kennel Club (AKC)**
Phone: 212-696-8200
Web site: *www.akc.org*

**American Society for the Prevention of Cruelty to Animals (ASPCA)**
Phone: 212-876-7700
Web site: *www.aspca.org*
E-mail: *information@aspca.org*

**The Association of Pet Dog Trainers (APDT)**
Phone: 800-738-3647
Web site: *www.apdt.com*
E-mail: information@apdt.com

**Delta Society**
Phone: 425-226-7357
Web site: *www.deltasociety.org*
E-mail: *info@deltasociety.org*

**Therapy Dogs International**
Phone: 973-252-9800
Web site: *www.tdi-dog.org*
E-mail: *tdi@gti.net*

**United Kennel Club**
Phone: 269-343-9020
E-mail: *pbickell@ukcdogs.com* (general registration questions)
Web site: *www.ukcdogs.com*

**Whole-Dog-Journal.com**
Phone: 800-829-9165
E-mail: *WholeDogJ@aol.com*
Web site: *www.whole-dog-journal.com*

## Canine Health

**Alternative Veterinary Medicine Web Site**
E-mail: wm010@altvetmed.com
Web site: *www.altvetmed.com*

**American Animal Hospital Association**
Phone: 303-986-2800
E-mail: healthypet@aahanet.com
Web site: *www.healthypet.com*

**American College of Veterinary Internal Medicine**
Phone: 303-231-9933
E-mail: acvim@acvim.org
Web site: *www.acvim.org*

**American Holistic Veterinary Medical Association**
Phone: 410-569-0795
E-mail: office@ahvma.org
Web site: *www.ahvma.org*

**The American Veterinary Medical Association**
Phone: 847-925-8070
E-mail: avmainfo@avma.org
Web site: *www.avma.org*

# Dog Activities

**Canine Freestyle Federation**
E-mail: directors@canine-freestyle.org
Web site: *www.canine-freestyle.org*

**Flyball Home Page**
Web site: *www.flyballdogs.com*

**International Sled Dog Racing Association**
E-mail: dsteele@brainerd.net
Web site: *www.isdra.org*

**National Association for Search and Rescue**
Phone: 703-222-6277
E-mail: Info@NASAR.org
Web site: *www.nasar.org*

**National Urban Search and Rescue Response System**
Phone: 202-566-1600
Web site: *www.fema.gov/usr*

**North American Dog Agility Council**
E-mail: info@nadac.com
Web site: *www.nadac.com*

**North American Flyball Association**
Phone: 800-318-6312
Web site: *www.flyball.org*

**North American Hunting Retriever Association**
E-mail: nahra@nahra.org
Web site: *www.nahra.org*

**United States Dog Agility Association**
Phone: 972-487-2200
E-mail: info@usdaa.com
Web site: *www.usdaa.com*

**The World Canine Freestyle Organization**
Phone: 718-332-8336
E-mail: wcfodogs@aol.com
Web site: *www.worldcaninefreestyle.org*

## Equipment and Supplies

**Cherrybrook**
E-mail: custserv@cherrybrook.com
Web site: *www.cherrybrook.com*

**The Dog's Outfitter**
Phone: 800-367-3647
E-mail: customerservice@dogsoutfitter.com
Web site: *www.dogsoutfitter.com*

**Dogwise**
Phone: 800-776-2665
E-mail: mail@dogwise.com
Web site: *www.dogwise.com*

**J-B Wholesale Pet Supplies**
Phone: 800-526-0388
E-mail: customerservice@jbpet.com
Web site: *www.jbpet.com*

**KV Vet Supply**
Phone: 800-423-8211
Web site: *www.kvvet.com*

**Max 200 Agility and Obedience Equipment**
Phone: 800-446-2920
E-mail: info@max200.com
Web site: *www.max200.com*

**PetEdge**
Phone: 800-329-6372
E-mail: order@petedge.com
Web site: *www.petedge.com*

**SitStay.com**
Phone: 800-748-7829
Web site: *www.sitstay.com*

# Index

# Acknowledgments

Special thanks from Adams Media to all the dogs who appear throughout this book, and to their human families for supplying us with their photos: Lynda Warwick, Jen Stiles, and Molly; Karen Hocker and Dieffenbaker; Dawn Sullivan, Millie, and Scootchie; Carol Raheily and Max; Peggy McNally, Bo, Haley, and Cassie; and Gerilyn and Paul Bielakiewicz, Reggae, and Stryker.